PROTESTANTISM
AND PROGRESS

A HISTORICAL STUDY OF THE
RELATION OF PROTESTANTISM
TO THE MODERN WORLD

BY

ERNST TROELTSCH

TRANSLATED BY

W. MONTGOMERY, B.D.

Wipf and Stock Publishers
150 West Broadway • Eugene OR 97401

1999

The first English translation was published in 1912 and was first
published as a Beacon Paperback in 1958.

Protestantism and Progress
*A Historical Study of the Relation of Protestantism to the
Modern World*
By Troeltsch, Ernst

ISBN: 1-57910-226-3

Reprinted by *Wipf and Stock Publishers* 1999
150 West Broadway • Eugene OR 97401

PREFACE

THE publishers of the English translation of this little book of mine have requested me to write a special preface addressed to the English reader, and I have very willingly consented to do so. The purpose of such a preface can only be, I think, to say a word about the place which this book occupies in relation to my work as a whole, and, as it would argue a want of modesty in me to assume that the latter is widely known, briefly to indicate its general character.

In the aim which has guided my studies, two main interests may be distinguished. The first is that of gaining an insight into the intellectual and religious situation of the present day, from which the significance and the possibilities of development possessed by Christianity might be deduced.   That has led me to engage in historical investigations regarding the spirit of the modern world, for this can only be understood in the light of its relation to the earlier epochs of Christian civilisation in Europe. As Adolf Harnack has described the genesis and the disintegration of Christian dogma, so I should like to examine the present situation and its significance for the fate of Christianity in the modern world.   For anyone who holds the opinion that in spite of all the significance which Catholicism retains, the living possibilities of development and progress are to be found on Protestant soil, the question regarding the relation of Protestantism to modern civilisation becomes of high importance.   And the question is by no means to be answered in so simple a fashion as common opinion was, and is, accustomed to answer it.   It must be treated with complete objectivity and impartiality, and, so far as matters of fact are concerned, the results must be convincing alike for believers and unbelievers, Protestants and non-Protestants. The investigation must be strictly historical, and in no way biassed by theological prepossessions.

In regard to the other main interest, the matter stands differently. Taking the aforesaid survey of the situation as its basis, it endeavours to distinguish those elements in modern civilisation which have proved their value from those which are merely temporary and lead nowhere. It seeks further, and above all, to give to the religious ideas of Christianity —which I hold to be the sole really religious force in our European system of civilisation, and which I also believe to be superior to the religions of the East—a shape and form capable of doing justice to the absoluteness of religious conviction, and at the same time in harmony with the valuable elements in the modern spirit.   This department of my work is, of course, based on very personal and subjective, although at the same time carefully reasoned, convictions and presuppositions. Here, of course, it is impossible to look for the same general acceptability of results as in the previous case.   It is quite possible to follow me in the former, and part company with me in the latter.

The present book belongs distinctly to the former circle of interests, and personal religious views are carefully excluded from the purely historical analysis.   It was thus possible for a lecture which I was invited to deliver at the ninth Congress of German Historians to form the kernel of this book.   It gives the quintessence of my investigations on the special point of the relation of Protestantism to the Modern Spirit, and, by way of a strict examination of cause and effect, it seeks to determine how much the Modern Spirit actually owes to

Protestantism, and how much it has received from other sources, or, again, has produced as new from its own essence. Only when this purely causal investigation has been completed is a comparison entered upon between the essential character of Protestantism and the Modern Spirit, in order to determine how far community of idea, and how far opposition, is present, and how far the oppositions are reconcilable or otherwise.

Hence it is the essential characteristic of this book to treat the questions which it raises not merely on dogmatic and metaphysical, but also on practical grounds—ethical, political, and economic.

For every metaphysic has its roots, and must find its test, in practical life. In the result, this special way of approaching the problem leads us to assign to Anglo-Saxon Protestantism a significance corresponding not merely to its vast numerical preponderance, but also to what it has actually accomplished towards the solution of the practical problems of the Christian life.

Having said this, I believe I have given a sufficient indication of the purpose of the book. If any reader finds its spirit too purely objective or sceptical, I will only ask him to remember that this is not due to any lack of religious convictions on my part, but to the fact that I have thought it right to reserve their expression for another place.

ERNST TROELTSCH.

Heidelberg, 10*th September* 1912.

CONTENTS

PROTESTANTISM
AND PROGRESS

INTRODUCTION

No science can escape from the conditions imposed by the constitution of the thinking mind which gives it birth. Even History, for all its striving after exactitude, objectivity, and minuteness of investigation, does not escape from such conditions. These are summed up in the fact that we are constantly obliged to come back to present experience. The present continually hovers before the backward-looking glance, because it is by the aid of analogies drawn from the life of to-day—however little this may be consciously before the mind—that we reach the causal explanation of the events of the past. But what is still more important is that we always, either voluntarily or involuntarily, relate the course of past events to the complex of effects which lies before us in the present, and that we are constantly drawing either special or general conclusions from the past and making use of them in our task of shaping the present with a view to the future.

Subjects which do not admit of such a relation to the present belong to the antiquarian, and investigations which entirely and on principle leave such considerations out of account have value only for the virtuoso, or as work for work's sake.   Even when we employ the art, so familiar to modern thinking, of tracing out evolutionary series, we do so at bottom only in order that we may be able to understand the present itself in its place in such a series ; and when we follow the not less familiar tendency to construct historical laws out of these series, there lies in the background the wish to insert the " particular " of the present into the "general" of the whole course of things, in order that both present and future may be better understood.

Thus the understanding of the present is always the final goal of all history. History is just the whole life experience of our race, which we have to remember as long and as well, to apply to our present existence as well and as closely, as we can. Every historical investigation works tacitly with these co-efficients; and it is avowedly the highest goal of history wherever history is conscious of itself as an organic science with a definite significance for the whole of our knowledge.

Expressly to set oneself such a task implies, of course, an undertaking in which the constructive intelligence plays a part—the grasping together of the present under a general conception characteristic of its essence, and the comparison of this whole with the past as a group of historical factors and tendencies which have also to be described and characterised by general concepts. The fact is, that no historical investigation, be it as specialist as you please, can dispense with general conceptions of this kind; all it can do is to make the mistake of

thinking them self-explanatory. But when that
is done, the really important problems remain
latent in the supposed self-explanatory conceptions, and these must ever anew be made
the object of historical thought. Of course
the distinctively constructive and conceptual
character of such thought must be frankly
admitted. It takes detailed investigation as
its presupposition, and remains dependent
upon it; it has its own special dangers and
pitfalls in the way of false generalisation, and
should bear itself modestly towards strict
professional research. That, however, does
not alter the fact that it has constantly to
be freshly undertaken, and that in it real
historical thought finds its expression. It
alone makes it possible to group the already
worked-up material with a view to further
work, to trace out the connexions and to
interrogate the material afresh. It, above all,
makes possible the attainment of the chief
aim which is tacitly pursued by all history—
the understanding of the present. With all

its consciousness of the many sources of error
by which it is beset, it may confidently insist
upon its rights.

This constructive thought will not, indeed,
after the manner of the older theology,
meditate upon the ways of Providence, or,
like Hegel, trace out the necessary self-
unfolding of the Idea, or, again, like psychological positivism, reconstruct the necessary
causal succession of certain collective conditions, or mental and spiritual types. It
will only, while remaining entirely within the
limits of experience, formulate, so far as
possible, the various great factors of our
historical existence in general concepts, and
endeavour to throw light on the actual relations, causal and genetic, between the
aforesaid successive and overlapping types
of civilisation.[1] From these successions and

[1] [In the present work *Kultur* has been uniformly
rendered by "civilisation." The two words are not exact
equivalents. In the main they cover the same ground,
but they sum up the same phenomena from rather different
points of view. Both include a reference to the whole

intersections it has then to explain our modern world, to which we refer, for purposes of comparison or derivation, all historical knowledge, and which we desire to understand in its characteristic fundamental features, to the end that we may understand ourselves. All constructive work going beyond this in the direction of the philosophy of history belongs, not to history proper, but to philosophy, to metaphysics, to ethics, or to religious conviction. On the

conditions, mental, moral, and material, of a given stage of social development, but the English word suggests *primarily* a reference to the social organisation, as the sphere within which the other features develop; the German suggests *primarily* a reference to the stage of intellectual and ethical development, as the source from which the other features proceed. This difference of orientation sometimes makes the one term slightly less natural in a combination of ideas entirely appropriate to the other, but, on the whole, they correspond satisfactorily enough. In certain specialist writings, particularly in Anthropology, "culture" is freely used in the German sense, but as the word is already in use in current English with an allied but much more restricted meaning (= German *Bildung*), it does not seem desirable to adopt this usage in works of a more general character.—Translator.]

strictly *a posteriori* lines, however, which have just been indicated, constructive work of this kind belongs to history proper, and it is only on these empirical lines that the following attempt at such construction is planned.[1]

[1] Felix Rachfahl has felt it necessary to raise a protest, in the name of genuine professional history, against my constructions, by attacking in his characteristically pedantic and dictatorial fashion Max Weber's essay on Calvinism— to which I shall have occasion to refer later on—and in conjunction with it the present lecture, as well as my work in *Kultur der Gegenwart* (*cf.* "Kapitalismus und Kalvinismus" in the *Internationale Wochenschrift* for 1909, and "Nochmals Kapitalismus and Kalvinismus" in the same periodical for 1910). He pronounces that my historical constructions are "nothing but ill-considered and ill-judged generalisations based on insufficient knowledge of the subject," etc. I have no desire or intention to follow him in this vein; specific points have been answered in my *Sociallehren.* [The author's large work on the Social Teachings of the Christian Churches.] I have only to remark that his knowledge in matters of economic history and theory, and especially in matters of theology and the history of religion, is certainly not such as to make his superior attitude appear well considered and well judged. He is himself a clear illustration of the fact that alongside of professional, specialised research—I have nothing against its being given a long way the first place—there is ample room for the tracing out of the great thought-forces of history, for which, of course, some knowledge is a necessary pre-requisite. In truth, the two kinds of work ought to

supplement and fructify one another. Instead of that,
Rachfahl indulges in all kinds of gibes, which evidently
appear to him very witty, against the "constructionists."
I, for my part, have no objection to give due weight to
Rachfahl's criticism where it appears to me justified.
What I have to correct is not indeed very much ; see my
reply, "Die Kulturbedeutung des Calvinismus" in the
Internationale Wochenschrift for 1910.

CHAPTER I

The Meaning of "The Modern World"

Of the historical conceptions with which our inquiry has to deal, one which is apparently among the simplest, but in reality is often rather loosely used, is that of the "modern world"—or, if we wish to avoid the pretentious term "world," which extends rather unduly the sphere of our own existence, the conception of modern civilisation as developed in Europe and America. It will be advisable at the outset to seek a more exact definition of this term, for when this is found it will suggest to us the questions which we shall have to put to Protestantism as one of the ancestors of modern civilisation. This civilisation, of course, includes within itself the most

various tendencies, but it bears nevertheless a
certain general stamp, of which we are instinc-
tively conscious. The designation "modern"
is in this connection to be understood only
a potiori, since it continues to include a large
proportion of the older factors; but it is precisely in the struggle with these older factors
that it becomes conscious of its individuality.
This individuality, however, is very difficult to
define, partly because of the manifoldness and
heterogeneity of the factors and conditions
which characterise it, partly because of the
want of a strict *differentia*, such as might be
afforded when the contrast with a different
subsequent civilisation had made it possible
to recognise the forces which, at the close
quarters of present experience, cannot all be
brought into the field of vision, or, at any rate,
do not fall into proper perspective. We are
therefore, for the most part, reduced to defining it by contrast with preceding periods,
especially with the immediately preceding
period, of civilisation. Thus the characteristics

by which we have to define it are essentially
negative. Modern civilisation, indeed, first
became conscious of its newness by its
antithetic relation to that which preceded it;
while its attempts to produce something new
took the most varied forms. And even at the
present day a general characterisation of it
can only be given by negative determinations
of this kind.

Modern civilisation, if we look to its immediate context, took its rise from the great
period of Church-civilisation, based on the
belief in an absolute and immediate Divine
revelation and the embodiment of this
revelation in the Church as the organ of
redemption and moral discipline. There
is nothing which can be compared with the
power of such a faith when it is really
a natural growth, and stands unquestioned.
For when this is the case, God, the Divine
will, is everywhere, immediately present,
exactly recognisable, having as its organ an
infallible institution. In these conditions all

strength for great achievements and all assurance regarding the ultimate goal of life are
drawn from this revelation and its organised
expression in the Church. The creation of
this mighty edifice was the last effort of
antiquity, under the decisive influence of
Christianity ; and this edifice forms the centre
of what is known as medieval civilisation.
The immediate intrusion into the world of the
Divine, with its laws, forces, and ends, exactly
definable against the background of purely
natural capacity, determines everything, and
produces an ideal of civilisation which, in
theory at least, signifies a direction of mankind as a whole by the Church and its
authority—an ideal which everywhere authoritatively determines the mode of combination
of supernatural, Divine, with natural, earthly,
human ends.   Supreme over all is the *Lex
Dei*, which is composed of the *Lex Mosis* or the
Decalogue in combination with the *Lex Christi*
and the *Lex Ecclesiæ*, but also as *Lex Naturæ*
includes within itself the juridico-ethical and

the scientific heritage of antiquity, and the natural claims of life.

The great theory which regulates everything is this. At bottom both laws, the biblico-ecclesiastical, and the Stoic, natural, law, are one, since in their original form they coincided. It is only now, in sinful humanity, that they diverge ; and under the direction of the Church their proper equivalence is again to be restored, though now, indeed, conditioned by the continuance of original sin.

It is, therefore, above all things a *civilisation of authority* in the fullest sense, arousing, by its authority, the highest aspirations after eternal salvation, stirring the most living depths of subjective soul-life, and uniting the immutable Divine with the mutable human in a cosmos of ordered and organised functions. Moreover, this religious authority leads men, by means of the Church's ordinances of salvation, up from the present world, corrupted as it is by original sin, to the other and higher world. The consequence of this is the de-

preciation of the earthly sensuous world and
the fundamentally ascetic character of the
whole theory and shaping of life. This
asceticism has sometimes the primarily mystical sense of an extinguishing of all that is
finite and sensuous in the eternal and super-
sensuous ; sometimes primarily the disciplinary
sense of a methodical adaptation and direction
of all action towards the ends of the other life.
In the former case it tends to Quietism; in
the latter to methodical action. Catholicism
practised both : in pattern form among the
clergy and the religious orders ; and among the
laity with due regard to the conditions of the
practical life. Further points that have to be
noticed are, that, alongside of all this, real life
made good its claims ; and that both Christian
theism, and also the heritage received from
ancient civilisation, represented another way of
regarding the world.

These contradictory tendencies were recon-
ciled by the Church in the system of spiritual
and secular functions which it created. In

this system the consistent carrying out of the ascetic method of life is confined to the official representatives of the Church, the clergy, and those who voluntarily dedicate themselves to this ideal, the monastic orders, while under their direction the mass of the people, of whom they are the representatives and spiritual guides, perform their various social functions according to the *Lex Naturæ*, being only subjected to the ascetic ideal from time to time, or in a limited degree. Just as the authority of the Church knew how to recognise alongside of it the natural reason, so asceticism was able to take under its wing the natural life. Catholicism is therefore characterised by an extremely elastic union of the ascetic life prescribed by authority and the freer natural life " in the world," and in this union it organised the civilisation of the whole of later antiquity, and, to a still greater extent, of the Romano-Germanic so-called Middle Ages. Its whole outlook on the world and its whole dogmatic system, its science, its ethics,

its political and social doctrines, its juridical
and economic theories, and the whole of its
practical activities, are dominated by this
point of view.   No importance is attached to
the independent discovery of new truths ; nor
is a new political and social edifice to be
constructed by conscious organising effort.
The ideal is simply that the established truths,
natural and revealed, the Church's dominion
over the world and the politico-social conditions which unalterably result from the nature
of things, are to be brought into a harmony
dominated by the religious ends of life, and
regulated both directly and indirectly by
sacerdotal authority.   It is, when all is said
and done, a compromise, but a compromise
dominated by the authoritative, ascetic, world-
condemning, religious influences of the Church
as the organ of salvation.   Of course, the factors
we have indicated are not the only determining
factors of the Middle Ages.   There come in all
kinds of external conditions quite independent
of them, and in part necessary preliminaries to

the victory of the Church's scheme of civilisation. Such were, the political and social situation in late antiquity, the juridical and economic conditions obtaining among the Germanic races, the opportunity for Church direction in the rudimentary economic conditions of the early Middle Ages, the restriction, in the early days of city life, of trade and industry by the corporate form of their organisation, and the weakness of all central authority, apart from which the dominance of the Church would not have been possible. But the fact that all these conditions contributed to produce a Church-directed civilisation, finds after all its main explanation in the spiritual content and character of the latter, and therefore, as a whole, it may be characterised as the period of essentially Church civilisation.

In contrast with this the essential character of modern civilisation becomes apparent. It is everywhere engaged in opposing Church civilisation and in substituting for it ideals of civilisation independently arrived at, the authority of which depends on their inherent and immediate capacity to produce conviction. This independence, whatever its basis, as opposed to Church authority, to purely external divinely-given standards, dominates everything.   Even where new authorities are in principle established, or in practice followed, the respect accorded to them arises from purely independent and rational conviction; and even where the older religious convictions hold their ground, their truth and their binding force are, at least among Protestants, primarily based on inner personal conviction, not on submission to authority as such.

Only strict Catholicism stands by the old idea of authority, and is therein felt to be an intrusion into the modern world of a foreign body of anomalous character; and even Catholicism has been obliged to give up in many respects the practical implications of the claim.   The immediate consequence of such independence is necessarily a constantly growing individualism of conviction, opinion, theory, and practical aim. A bond of union absolutely superior to individualism can only be supplied by a power as tremendous as that of the belief in an immediate supernatural Divine revelation, such as Catholicism possessed, and organised in the Church as the extension and continuation of the Divine incarnation. Once this bond of union disappears, the immediate consequence is a splitting up, on the basis of all kinds of human opinions. These cannot pronounce decisions with absolute, Divine, but only with relative, human authority ; and however rationally based this human authority may feel itself to be, and however confidently it may hope to unite men on the basis of reason, there will always be a divergence among the various views and utterances of reason. Divine infallibility and ecclesiastical intolerance necessarily give place to human relativity and toleration.

When an endeavour was made to find objective standards and fixed points to oppose

to mere subjective caprice, scientific thought
presented itself as the only resource. In virtue
of its foundation in natural science, which was
in principle new in relation to antiquity and
its products, it offered new potentialities for
the establishment of a clearly and methodically
defined point of view, as well as for the
technical mastery of nature. In the place of
revelation, reigned scientific thought, and in
place of ecclesiastical authority, the literature
inspired by the new methods. Hence the
rationalistic, scientific character of modern
civilisation, in which its individualism both
freely expressed itself, and at the same time
seemed to find its natural boundaries. The
successor of theology, at once its contrast and
its counterpart, was found in the naturalistic,
rationalistic system of the sciences and the
regulation of life by the so-called Rationalism.

Of course, Individualism could not be always
and everywhere kept within these boundaries.
The more the supposedly fixed rational order
was made the object of historical thought,

with reference to its origin, and the more historical thought extended itself in the process beyond scientific thought in the narrower sense, the more completely was the fixed system dissolved into the flux of transience, with ever greater future possibilities opening before it. The independence of thought which came in along with Rationalism finally recognised that everything which was ostensibly rational was historically conditioned, and discovered the wide range of variation in professedly rational conceptions. This rationalistic Individualism passed more and more into a Relativism, the disruptive and divisive effects of which are only too familiar to us to-day, but in which we also recognise a liberation of the most tremendous forces and possibilities.

There are not wanting, of course, socialising reactions against this divisive tendency, both in theory and, more especially, in the practical phenomena of political and economic life. But these reactions rest on a different basis from

the Church's "authority" civilisation. Only
temporarily, in the period of the anti-rationalist
reaction, have the two movements approached
and coalesced with one another. Since then
they have again diverged. To-day it may
be said that the politico-economic counter-
movement against autonomous Individualism
daily becomes more widely separated from
that associated with the Church reaction.
For the former movement, like that which
it opposes, really rests upon the modern
principle of the autonomous and conscious
creation of human society, in a free form
suitable to changing conditions. It is not
revelation and the life to come which form
the strength of the prevailing modern forces
of association.

From all this results a further characteristic
of modern civilisation : the limitation of the
interests of life to the present world. If the
absolute authority has fallen, which, in its
absoluteness, made the antithesis of the
Divine and human equally absolute, if in

man an autonomous principle is recognised as the source of truth and moral conduct, then all conceptions of the world which were especially designed to maintain that gulf between the Divine and human, fall along with it. With it falls the doctrine of the absolute corruption of mankind through original sin, and the transference of the ends of life to the heavenly world in which there will be deliverance from this corruption. In consequence, all the factors of the present life acquire an enhanced value and a higher impressiveness, and the ends of life fall more and more within the realm of the present world and its ideal transformation.

Now, whether this tendency issues in pure secularism, or whether it holds to a connection, now of course inward and organic, between the doings of the present life and the continuation of life in the world to come, in any case the presuppositions of ecclesiastical asceticism have disappeared. We can now, as Lessing said, look forward to the future life as to the

morrow which naturally succeeds to-day.
Since it is no longer possible to separate and
mark off from one another the purely earthly
life and the life led by the power of God, life
appears either as purely human, or as filled in
its whole extent with the Spirit of God ; which
often enough works out in the end to much
the same result.   Pantheistic feeling is woven
into the texture of modern life, and expresses
itself in its Art and Science.   Whatever of
purely philosophic and scientific difficulty and
contradiction it may contain, it is in any case
the expression of a spirit of world-affirmation
with which the asceticism of the older type
of religious life is not reconcilable in any of
its aspects.   Religious asceticism in the form
of negation of the world and self-disciplining
with a view to a super-earthly life-aim has
disappeared from the modern world, however
completely the unrestrained enjoyment of life
has remained for it mere theory, and however
much the simple life of natural impulse has
been limited by reflection and purposeful work.

And with this is connected the final characteristic of the modern spirit—its self-confident optimism and belief in progress. This was an accompanying phenomenon of the struggle for freedom in the period of Illuminism, which without such a confidence could not have broken the old chains, and it then found confirmation in a multitude of discoveries and new creations. The old cosmic conceptions dominated by the Fall, the redemption of the world, and the final Judgment have fallen away. To-day everything is filled with the thought of development and of progress upward from the depths of darkness to unknown heights. The despairing sense of sin, the sense of a great world-suffering imposed on us for our purification and punishment—the two presuppositions of redemption and the Church's ordinances of redemption—have been banished. And even where the progressive spirit falters, and the misery of the world makes itself felt, it is no longer the old Christian pessimism based on the Fall, but a scepticism based on experience, or on a pessimistic metaphysic. That is not to say that all the forces of the religious life of Israel and of Christianity have been cut off at the roots. But in comparison with their former power to provide a basis for the saving ordinances of the authoritative Church with its discipline and training for the other world, they have certainly become extraordinarily weak and lifeless. They are no longer capable of producing or sustaining a Church-directed civilisation.

To these characteristic marks of the modern spirit have to be added those which belong to the domain of purely practical circumstances and conditions; in regard to which it is difficult to say how far they determine that spirit or are on the other hand determined by it. There is the whole phenomenon of the formation of giant states with their vast military power, which shatters the dream of an ecclesiastical world-empire, the development of modern capitalistic business-organisation, bringing everything under its sway, the growth of applied science, which has accomplished more in a couple of centuries than in the two previous millenniums, the immense increase in the figures of population, which has become possible through all this and in turn creates the necessity of it all, the bringing of the whole world within our mental horizon and the contact with immense non-Christian empires, the struggles of the nations without, in the arena of world-politics, and the struggle within of the new social classes created by this development. All this combines with the mental and spiritual revolutions described above to form a new whole, which brings with it new duties and problems, as compared with the ancient world of Church civilisation; in which the old Churches, their worldview and their ethics have no longer any firm basis, however strongly the indestructible religious yearning and the need for a fixed point of support may make men cling to the remnants of the ancient ecclesiastical

world, which still retain no inconsiderable
influence.[1]

[1] The most learned and instructive criticism of the
present lecture, Loofs's rectorial address on "Luther's
Relation to the Middle Ages and to Modern Times," 1907,
opposes itself especially to this description of the modern
world and the consequent antithesis between the world
of the Reformation and that of to-day.   "Between Luther
and the modern world there is no such great gulf fixed
as Troeltsch here assumes.   Had we not ourselves until
1874 compulsory baptism?   And is not blasphemy still
punishable by law?   And have we not still to-day a civilisation of authority, of a Christian colouring, with, broadly
speaking, obligatory religious instruction?   Materially the
conception of blasphemy is now no doubt very different
from that of Luther.   But in a *formal* aspect the difference
of the periods is not so great as the enlightened reader
might suppose when he shudders at the thought of the
ecclesiastical civilisation of compulsion" (p. 19).   That is
true, especially as regards Prussia, but it seems to me a
poor consolation.   Loofs goes on to say : "Some individuals,
indeed I am prepared to admit, in university circles
perhaps a majority, share Troeltsch's view regarding
supernaturalism, etc.   But even if they were right, the
fact would remain that they are not the modern world,
much less an incarnation of what the modern world has
thought for the last 200 years.   The modern world as
Troeltsch constructs it is present in certain—in some
cases numerous—circles, but the decisive battle between
the religion of the present world, consisting of pantheistic
conceptions of immanence, and the tradition of a living
theism has not yet been fought.   The modern period,

There are not wanting those who profess to see in this modern world chiefly the signs of the dissolution of an old, firmly-constructed, deeply-rooted civilisation. People have been ready to compare it with that period of civilisation which falls at the beginning of our Era.

with which Luther stands in such strong contrast according to Troeltsch's description, is so far from having begun 200 years ago that it is not yet completely born" (p. 24). That is not correct, for it is not a mere question of pantheism and university professors. And the examples at which Loofs eagerly clutches (p. 23) as indications of the continuance of an essential homogeneity between the world of the Reformers and the modern world are in my estimation mere straws. Especially, to appeal to Kant and Goethe in testimony to the persistence of the idea of original sin is a very doubtful procedure. Kant's doctrine of radical evil will only fit into the frame of a very modern non-ecclesiastical religious philosophy—such as Kant's in fact was; and Goethe declared in regard to Kant, that "after spending a long lifetime in cleansing his philosopher's cloak from many dirty prejudices, he had wantonly defiled it with the shameful stain of radical evil, in order that Christians also might be drawn to kiss its hem" (*Joh. Kasp. Lavater*, Zurich, 1902, p. 346). Kant and Goethe indeed show with characteristic clearness the spiritual traits of the modern world. What they have in common with the Reformers appears with new meaning and in a new form, and, above all, in a fundamentally different general context.

Out of that period Church civilisation arose, renewing and re-creating it by the infusion of new ideas and new blood. But apart from this renewal, in its individualistic autonomous rationalism, so closely resembling that of the present day, and in the vacillating uncertainty of religious and moral conviction, it represented the dissolution of the ancient Mediterranean civilisation.

Precisely this comparison with late antiquity, however, serves, after all, to indicate those features of the modern spirit which are of a positive character—whereas, when compared with the Church civilisation of the Middle Ages, it had chiefly to be distinguished by negative and formal characteristics. In the modern world there meets us everywhere, instead of dissolution, a thronging host of new creations. Instead of a helplessness taking refuge in phantasy and scepticism, we find in the modern world an imposing and constantly increasing practical mastery of things. In the first place, there appears instead of the universal monarchy of antiquity, with its deadening effect upon individual life, the system of great national states with extensive territories, standing, or desiring to stand, in equipoise; also a political organisation of these states which gives to the citizens a share in their government, not directly by the primitive universal assembly, but by systems of representation; further, a juridical, bureaucratic, and military organisation of these states, which gives them a peculiar solidity, and brings the ends of civilisation in their widest extent within the ends of the State. Finally, in place of a horizon bounded by the Mediterranean coasts, we have now an ocean horizon, which offers immensely greater and more involved problems of expansion and colonisation. Everywhere that means new tasks, which are still far enough from being accomplished. In the second place, we observe a condition of economic life which opens up much wider possibilities; which, no longer based on household and slave production, but upon a highly

organised national economy, upon a system
of international exchange made possible by
currency and credit, upon a fabulous development of applied science, and, above all, upon
capitalism, affords to a formally and legally
free population opportunities for the almost
limitless exploitation of all its powers and
gifts.   From all these conditions there results
an entirely new social classification, which,
alongside of political and military officialdom,
has produced the wholly new phenomenon
of a capital-owning and cultured middle-class,
and puts the free working population in a
position to strive, not only for a formal legal
equality, but also for an equal share of
material benefits.   That does not look like an
end, but rather like a beginning, of great
social developments.

In particular, the kernel of the social life
is formed by a family life in which monogamy
is expressly raised to an ethical principle, the
sexes stand in an independent personal and
legal relation towards one another, love is

refined by romanticism and sensibility, the *patria potestas* in regard to the children is relaxed, and the mutual cohesion of the " clan " or wider family is very much diminished. This sexual ethic of the monogamic family —no easy thing to establish and maintain— implies a capacity for constant rejuvenation, a fountain of youth for the renewal of ethical energy.

To take yet a third point. The modern world possesses a wealth of knowledge which no doubt connects with the heritage derived from antiquity, and especially with the stronger emphasis laid on this at the so-called Renaissance; but it, nevertheless, starting from the vantage ground of an infinitely wider experience, goes far beyond this inherited knowledge and its categories of thought, possessing quite a new grasp of reality, and it has before it in the future a task to which no limits can be set. Moreover, this knowledge has become, through popular education and the printing press, a really practical power, an aid

in the struggle for existence available for
everyone. In the department of natural
science it has rationalised Nature to an extent
and degree which justify us in speaking of a
real domination of nature by spirit, and
enables the practical arts, freed from empirical
and unintelligent routine and resting upon
the knowledge of natural law, to advance
by incessant new invention and further development. In the department of historical
science it has so fully and thoroughly worked
out the genesis of our civilisation, and has
so made all present conditions intelligible by
tracing the history of their development, that
all thinking is obliged to become in some
measure historical, and that this knowledge
is an essential part of the equipment of all
attempts to modify present conditions. The
consequence of all this is, of course, a certain
Relativism, a mental complexity, and the
possession of a wealth of analogies for all
kinds of comparison such as no other period
has ever known. At the same time, however,

a strong sense of continuity prevents any paralysing effect from resulting, and the idea of original tasks belonging to the present age does not die out. The conception of ourselves as the heirs of a great historical whole, to which we have to contribute, stimulates energy, and teaches us to use the experiences of the past and to regard the future as the · offspring of the present, for which we are responsible to our successors.

Last, but not least, the modern world is characterised by the fact that its Individualism is of a much more deeply and strongly rooted metaphysical constitution. It is not a mere continuation and extension of the ancient rationalism or the ancient scepticism. Neither is it the spiritualistic temper of Platonism and the later Stoicism, which, entering into an intimate union with Christianity, have accompanied it throughout. No doubt both were renewed at the Renaissance so far as they had not already been preserved by their amalgamation with Christianity, and from

that point forward have exercised a strong
influence down to the present day. But
modern Individualism is not primarily based
on the Renaissance. It is based, rather, on
the idea, which is essentially Christian, of the
destination of man to acquire perfected personality through the ascent to God as the source
both of all personal life and also of the world
—an ascent which therefore consists in a being
laid hold of and moulded by the Divine Spirit.
It is the metaphysic, herein implied, of absolute
Personality, which directly, or indirectly, per-
meates our whole world and gives to the
thought of freedom, of personality, of the
autonomous self, a metaphysical background,
which has its influence even when it is
contested or denied. This spiritual temper
was founded by Christianity and the Israelitish
prophetism. Later, Christianity drew into
and fused with itself Platonism and Stoicism.
It held together and renewed antiquity in
its decline, by calling forth as its last product
the divinely-constituted State, the Church,

and the world-empire of personalities having their basis and union in God. The spiritual temper of Christianity, thus expanded, was in growing measure communicated by Catholicism to the Barbarians who created the civilisation of the Middle Ages, its communication being facilitated by their own politico-social institutions. It also, from the time of the Franciscan movement, prepared the way for Renaissance sentiment, and formed the strongest root of its " individualised " civilisation. Finally, Protestantism has consciously and definitely formulated it as a principle, loosed it from its connection with a hierarchic world-dominating institution, and made it capable of freely combining with all the interests and factors of life.

Thus, in contrast with late antiquity and the Middle Ages, the special character of modern civilisation becomes sufficiently evident. At the same time we see clearly the influences and elements contributed by each of the various concrete historical factors to the for-

mation of the world of to-day. And thus
becomes manifest its quite extraordinary complexity. We recognise in it, antiquity and
Catholicism, the social and political characteristics of the Romano-Germanic peoples, the
rise of modern commerce and capitalism, the
differentiation of nationalities in the late
Middle Ages, colonial and maritime expansion,
the Renaissance, the modern sciences, modern
art and æstheticism, Protestantism. Hence
are derived the materials with which modern
individualistic Rationalism works. It is not,
however, itself derived from criticism and
intellectual emancipation, but has its deepest
root in a metaphysic and ethic which have
been deeply implanted into the spirit of our
whole modern civilisation by Christianity—by
late antiquity only in its fusion with Christianity. On this point we must not allow ourselves to be deceived by all the hostility to
the Churches and to Christianity, by all the
naturalistic or æsthetic pantheism, which
prevail at the present day. The present-day

world does not live by logical consistency, any more than any other; spiritual forces can exercise a dominant influence even where they are avowedly opposed. Were it not for the religious Personalism which we have had ingrained into us by prophetism and Christianity, individual autonomy, the belief in progress, the all-embracing community of mental outlook, the indestructibility and strength of our confidence in life and of our impulse to work, would be impossible. Our world affirms these ideas in their main extent, with, doubtless, a consciousness that they are in some way Christian, and even where it denies or ignores them, nevertheless shows traces of their influence.[1]

This gives us the most general point of view from which our question may be answered.

[1] Since my first edition I have made several attempts to reformulate these ideas in various ways. See "Das Wesen des modernen Geistes" in the *Preuss. Jahrb.* for 1907; "Autonomie und Rationalismus in der modernen Welt," *Internationale Wochenschrift* for 1907; "Das stoisch-christliche Naturrecht und das profane Naturrecht," *Hist. Zeitschrift*, vol. cvi., 1911.

Since Protestantism has a special significance for the development of this religious Individualism and its extension to the whole range of common life, it is clear from the outset that it has had no inconsiderable influence in producing the modern world. And this has always been recognised, whether as a matter for praise or blame, except by those who wish to derive the whole origin of the modern world from the Renaissance, or even from the age of the positive sciences which succeeded it. And, of course, the significance of Protestantism must not be exaggerated. A large part of the basis of the modern world, in the departments of the State, society, economics, science and art, arose quite independently of Protestantism, and has been produced partly by a simple continuance of the developments of the late Middle Ages, partly by the influence of the Renaissance, and especially by the Renaissance as modified by Protestantism, partly by the Catholic nations like Spain, Austria, Italy, and especially France, after the rise of Protestantism and independently of it. Nevertheless, the great significance of Protestantism for the arising of the modern world is incontestable. The important question is only wherein, in detail, this significance actually consists. On this point there prevail among scholars, and still more in the popular literature, very diverse and very inaccurate ideas. Catholic literature is accustomed to see in it the roots of the revolutionary spirit in the modern world. Treitschke's famous oration on Luther of 1883 sees in it the very source of all that is great and noble in the modern world. In the Hegelian school it is customary to extol it as the ethic and religion of immanence. In the Ritschlian school it appears as the creator of the family, the State, society, and organised avocations in the modern sense. The ordinary Catholic-Protestant apologetic and polemic in both camps makes play with the loosest generalisations, the one party seeing in Protestantism only the disintegrating, the other only the renewing and solidifying, agency, in reference to the true ordering of life.   But the matter is really not by any means so simple. It is a highly complex problem, in which scholarship in general is only in the process of rightly perceiving and formulating the individual questions.   It is in many cases still far enough from finding a proper answer to them.

The survey of these problems which will be offered in the following pages can therefore often give nothing more than conjectures and suggestions.   Only by the co-operation of scholars in very different departments will it be possible to find complete solutions.

CHAPTER II

THE MEANING OF "PROTESTANTISM"

IN "Protestantism" we have, of course, once
more a historical general-conception which
imperatively calls for more exact definition.
The prevalent custom is to resume under this
term all the phenomena which fall within the
sphere of Protestant religion down to the present day, and then to found on these a general
conception which represents rather what Protestantism might be or might become than what
it actually is. Thus there usually predominates
in these definitions either the conception of an
orthodoxy which has become weakened down
and lost hold of fixed principles, or of a develop-
ing and transforming philosophic outlook. In
the one case as in the other, however, it is no
longer a question of *a posteriori* historical

general conceptions which exhibit the real
state of the case as a whole, but of ideal conceptions which, attaching themselves to the
real, emphasise one or the other element in it,
and thereby seek to justify their formula as giving its " essence " or " fundamental tendency."

Such ideal conceptions are, of course, indispensable to present action and volition,
but they are by no means historical general-
conceptions of the kind that we are in search
of.[1] If we are seeking a purely historical
definition of Protestantism, we soon recognise
that, for Protestantism as a whole, it cannot
be immediately formulated. For modern Protestantism as a whole, even when it carries on
the orthodox dogmatic traditions, is in point of
fact completely changed. The genuine early
Protestantism of Lutheranism and Calvinism

---

[1] On the character of such "historical general-concep-
tions," *cf.* my article, " Was heisst ' Wesen des Christen-
tums ' ? " in the *Christliche Welt* for 1903. Everyone
who is familiar with the subject will recognise that
my formulation of the concept is based on Rickert's
Methodenlehre.

is, as an organic whole, in spite of its anti-
Catholic doctrine of salvation, entirely a Church
civilisation like that of the Middle Ages. It
claims to regulate State and society, science and
education, law, commerce and industry, according to the supernatural standpoint of revelation,
and, exactly like the Middle Ages, everywhere
subsumes under itself the *Lex Naturæ* as being
originally identical with the Law of God.
Modern Protestantism, since the end of the
seventeenth century, has, on the contrary,
everywhere accepted the principle of the
State's recognising religious equality, or even
remaining religiously indifferent, and has in
principle handed over religious organisation
and the formation of religious associations to
voluntary effort and personal conviction, recognising in principle the possibility of a plurality
of different religious convictions and religious
societies existing alongside of one another. It
has further, in principle, recognised alongside
itself a completely untrammelled secular life,
which it no longer attempts to control, either

directly or indirectly, through the agency of
the State. In connexion with this it has
forgotten its former doctrine—which made
possible and encouraged this control—of the
identity of the *Lex Dei* and *Lex Naturæ*; so
completely forgotten it as to have lost all
understanding of it.

These are fundamental differences. They
have naturally manifested themselves also
in dogmatic upheavals and transformations,
especially in the transformation of the conceptions of Church and State, and in the
modification of the old absolute authority,
of the purely supernatural character, ascribed
to the Bible, a modification which has gone so
far that it has completely transformed the old
doctrines of revelation and redemption, which
were the determining factors of the whole
system.   If this is taken into account, we are
certainly justified, from a purely historical
point of view and especially from that of the
formulation of our problem, in drawing a distinction between early and modern Protest-

antism. Early Protestantism, in spite of its universal priesthood of believers and its principle of inwardness, has to be conceived as a strictly ecclesiastical supernaturalistic civilisation resting on an immediate authority with a strictly defined sphere, distinct from the world and its interests. Indeed, it actually endeavoured to carry through by its own methods this tendency of medieval civilisation more strictly, inwardly, and personally than it had been possible for the hierarchically constituted Church of the Middle Ages to do. The place of this hierarchy, as perpetuating the incarnation of Christ, was taken by the miraculous, all-accomplishing power of the Bible — the Protestant perpetuation of the Divine incarnation. The civil power saw to it that, at least externally, this Divine revelation encountered no contradiction, and that it came in contact with every man so as to exercise its purely inward and personal redemptive influence. The authority and saving power of the Bible alone were held capable

of accomplishing what had been unattainable
by the bishops and the Pope in consequence
of the externality of the means which they
employed, and the secularisation of the Church
as an Institution.

But when once this is clearly recognised,
early Protestantism differentiates itself clearly
from those historical movements which were
proceeding alongside of it — which modern
Protestantism has more or less completely
taken up into itself, but which were inwardly
deeply distinguished from it and had an
independent influence of their own in history.
Such are the humanistic, historical, philological, and philosophical theology, the sectarian Anabaptist movement with its assertion
of the Church's independence of the State,
and the wholly individualistic, subjectivistic
Spiritualism.   Early Protestantism distinguished itself from all these sharply and with
cruel violence; and it did so, not merely from
short-sighted bitterness or theological dog-
matism, nor from opportunism or from the

narrow sympathies of a period of decline. In all its leaders, in a Luther, a Zwingli, a Calvin, from the beginning, it was conscious of an inherent and essential opposition to them. And the reason is that by these movements, however Christian they might be in principle, the very idea of a Church civilisation, the absolute certainty of the revelation which formed its basis, or, again, the claim which the Church always deduced from this to Christianise, more or less forcibly, life as a whole, was definitely denied. It was precisely the withdrawal of these people into small pietistic circles, their holding aloof from the State, and their abandonment of compulsion in religious matters, which was opposed to the principles of the Reformers; who were therein at one with Catholicism, that they could not hold a revelation to be a true revelation which did not subordinate everything human to the Divine. Luther's early and occasional spiritualistic inclinations were quickly suppressed by the logical inferences from the idea of the Church, and remained for

4

two centuries without influence.   The Church
as an external Institution, the certainty of the
Bible, and the clear direction, by the combination of Church and State, of society, or of the
undivided *Corpus Christianum* which each
Church established at least within the sphere
put under its jurisdiction by the civil government, came to form the main interest; and it
was precisely this main interest which was
threatened from various sides by their
opponents.   It was not until modern Protestantism had lost sight of the idea of a
universal Church-civilisation that it could
characterise as genuine Protestant principles,
the duty of historico-philological criticism, the
organisation of Churches formed by voluntary
association, independent of the State, and
the doctrine of revelation by inner personal
conviction and illumination.   The older
Protestantism disposed of these under the
categories of " Naturalism " on the one hand,
and " Fanaticism," "Enthusiasm," "Sectarianism," on the other ; and to-day, so far as it sur-

vives—after effectively accepting these heresies
—attacks their spirit all the more passionately.
For our present purpose this distinction is,
in fact, extremely important. Movements
very closely allied with Protestantism and yet
quite sharply distinguished from it — the
humanistic philological theology which ac-
quired a separate organisation in Arminianism
and Socinianism, the sectarian Baptist groups
which organised themselves under the banner
of either Catholicism or Protestantism, the
mystics and spiritualists, who are either completely isolated or attach to themselves only
a purely personal and literary following, and
do away with the whole Church conception
of revelation and redemption : all these have
an extremely high significance for the arising
of the modern world, and certainly cannot
without more ado be put down to the account of Protestantism. Towards the close of
the seventeenth century, after long and cruel
oppression, they had their hour in the history
of the world. Free-Churchism, philologico-

critical theology, the subordination of objective revelation to the practical ethico-religious content of life, an immediacy of the religious consciousness which turns the historical element into a mere means of self-stimulation, a subjectivism which makes little of cultus, ceremonial and ecclesiasticism, have since then irresistibly broken in upon the Protestant Churches, like a flood sweeping away the old landmarks.   There is no longer any question of a single-moulded Church civilisation, based on a creed, embracing the whole of society; and its former dogmatic foundations are, even within the Churches, and in conservative circles, in process of complete disintegration.[1]

Finally, we have still to emphasise the

[1] Loofs has taken particular exception to my view of the Anabaptists, and the close association of them with the spiritualists (*ut sup.* p. 15).   Walther Köhler, too, has repeatedly noted it as one of the unsatisfactory points in my view.   And they are partly right.   I have therefore gone into the problem thoroughly in my *Soziallehren,* and believe that I have really arrived at something essentially new and better on this question.   The alterations made in the text of the present edition are based on this—I cannot, of course, here enter into detail.

difference which appears, within early Protestantism, in the two Confessions, Lutheran
and Calvinistic. This is by no means solely due
to the different local conditions of civilisation
in which the two arose, but lies, in spite of the
essential agreement in their dogmatic basis,
in certain subtle differences of religious and
ethical thought, corresponding to differences
in the character and disposition of the leaders,
which were intensified to an extraordinary
degree by the difference of general conditions
in the two cases. They appear first as quite
subsidiary matters, but produce developments
which diverge so widely that it becomes hardly
possible to bring them under a common
formula, and that, for our purpose, not only
one but two "Protestantisms" have to be
taken into account. The significance of
Calvinism in reference to our problem differs
in important ways from that of Lutheranism,
and it is necessary to make a very accurate
psychological analysis to detect, in regard to
each detail, with which system it is connected.

In any case, their significance for the modern world lies in quite different directions; and as the development of Calvinism has led to its leaving behind Lutheranism, which has remained stationary, and becoming a great power in the world, in all matters of ethics, organisation, politics, and social questions, its practical influence is much the greater.

Of course, if one takes one's stand on a very lofty point of vantage, it is possible to make the attempt to bring all these pheno-mena — Lutheranism, Calvinism, humanistic Christianity, Baptist sects, and spiritualistic Individualism — under the common concept of Protestantism.   All these groups are united in their ultimate roots, the personalisation of religion and the setting up of the Bible as the sole standard of faith.   And, on the other hand, the course of historical development has brought the originally divergent streams once more into one bed.   Ultimately, there-fore, from the most general point of view, they may, no doubt, be regarded as together forming a single whole. But such a conception only becomes possible from the standpoint of modern Protestantism, in which the mutual adjustment or fusion of the various elements has taken place, and even from this standpoint the general conception of the whole is still very difficult to define.[1] And especially for our problem, to distinguish these different tendencies is much more important than to obliterate their differences

[1] An ingenious attempt of this description has been made by the Erlangen philosopher Leser in his—in general very friendly—criticism of this lecture. *Cf.* "Das protestantische Christentum als Kulturfaktor" in the *Jahrb. f. die evangelische Landeskirche Bayerns*, for 1907. "It is, as the Reformation in effect recognised, the great and characteristic thing *in every truth, and especially in the highest, that is, religious truth* into which Christianity leads us, that, immediately, in the interior of the personality access is possible to the whole of the divinely redemptive complex of living forces, and that, accordingly, beyond all visible links of connexion, a religious fellowship of a spiritual character manifests itself which has no need for a fellowship of an external authoritative character." I am myself quite prepared to say that. But, for our problem, it does not help us, for it is more appropriate to modern Protestantism than to early Protestantism, and is applicable also to the Stoicism and Platonism of the Renaissance period.

in a sufficiently elusive general conception. For it is only in relation to the older Protestantism in its various groups that there can be any question of an influence of Protestantism in producing modern civilisation; seeing that modern Protestantism is itself an element in modern civilisation, and has been deeply influenced by it. Our answer would have a false orientation from the outset if we were to start from a conception of Protestantism which dated back into the older Protestantism all, or the principal, characteristics of modern Protestantism as a factor in civilisation, and thus made the road from this imaginary construction to modern civilisation simple and easy for ourselves. Not less important is it to distinguish between the two Confessions; for that prevents us from treating the conception of Protestantism too much as a mere abstraction, and compels us to give due weight to the quite distinct influence exercised by the special concrete elements in its constitution as a real entity.

And it is of quite peculiar importance to treat on a separate footing the humanistic theology, the Baptist movements, and the spiritualistic mystics. These groups, in spite of their originally close relations with it, were as remote from early Protestantism as they have come near to later Protestantism, and it would be a complete mistake to take the Protestantism of our own day, which has been influenced and transformed by them, and is, moreover, exposed to the full pressure of the problems of modern life, as the more or less definite point of departure of the development of modern civilisation. That would be to bar the way to the understanding of the real influences of genuine Protestantism, and, moreover, to ascribe to it influences in the causation of the modern world, the credit of which unquestionably belongs to those much harassed and much calumniated movements. And, finally, it would be to ascribe to Protestantism the production of things which have not grown up on religious soil at all.

CHAPTER III

PROTESTANTISM AND THE MODERN WORLD: POINTS OF CONTRAST

BUT if this is the position of matters, it is evident that the significance of Protestantism which is now in question is far from being of a quite simple nature. There is no direct road leading from Protestant Church-civilisation to the modern civilisation independent of the Church. Its significance, while in general beyond question, must in many cases be an indirect, or even an involuntary one, and the common element which, for all that, unites the two must lie very far down in the hidden depths below the surface of its conscious thought. There can, of course, be no question of modern civilisation's having been produced simply and solely by Protestantism. All that comes into question is the latter's share therein. But even this share is nothing simple and homogeneous. It differs in different departments of civilisation, and in them all is something more or less complex and elusive. That is precisely what constitutes the peculiar fascination of the problem, and in order to make this intelligible the opposition between Protestantism and modern civilisation must first be indicated more exactly.

The point of primary importance is that, historically and theologically regarded, Protestantism—especially at the outset in Luther's reform of the Church—was, in the first place, simply a modification of Catholicism, in which the Catholic formulation of the problems was retained, while a different answer was given to them. It was only gradually that out of this new answer developed consequences of radical importance for the history of religion, and only when the breach with the first form of Protestantism occurred did it

new answer to old problems

appear how far these consequences went beyond a mere new answer to old problems.[1] That, however, only comes into question later. Protestantism was at first concerned only with the answer to the old question about *assurance of salvation,* which has as its pre-

---

[1] What the new element was which Luther introduced along with this answer, I have, in the meantime, tried once more to define in the essay *Luther und die moderne Welt* in vol. 1. of the series "Wissenschaft und Bildung" (Quelle und Meyer), 1908. The most important part of this has been embodied in the second edition of my work in *Kultur der Gegenwart.* It is there made clear that I by no means fail to recognise Luther's greatness and originality; indeed, I am essentially at one in my view of Luther with Loofs, and even with so fierce a controversialist as H. Böhmer (*Luther im Lichte der neueren Forschung,* 1906). The difference of opinion turns on the question how far this Lutheran gospel is consistent with the altered spiritual and material conditions of the present. I hold the opposition here to be very great, and, consequently, in my view what is common to Luther and the Middle Ages is much more strongly emphasised. But I do not think of this common element as an "intractible remainder of Catholicism" which present-day theology ought quietly to get rid of; I consider it to be due to a connexion in fundamental features between ancient and medieval thinking, which can be retained in the present day only arbitrarily, or thoughtlessly, having no longer a fixed point of attachment in it.

suppositions the existence of God, and His
personal and ethical being, and in general the
whole Biblical and medieval cosmology, and has
as its only and pressing problem, how, in the
face of the condemnation of all men to Hell
in consequence of original sin, and in view of
the weakness and nothingness of all human
and creaturely strength, deliverance from the
Judgment, eternal blessedness, and on earth a
peace of heart corresponding thereto, secure
in its hopes, can be obtained. This is,
through and through, the old question which
the teaching and discipline of Catholicism
had impressed more and more deeply upon
men's hearts. Protestantism, instead of point-
ing to the hierarchic redemptive organisation
of the Church and its priesthood, and to the
opus operatum of the sacraments, supported
by the will, answers the question by point-
ing to a simple radical and personal decision
to believe, which, if it be really made in
earnest, can assure itself, once for all, from
the supernatural Divine revelation of the

Bible, of the forgiveness of sins in Christ, and which, on the basis of this certainty, produces all the ethical consequences of re-conciliation with God and spiritual union with God. The decisive act of faith receives deliverance purely as an objective assurance of salvation, through the Bible, thus excluding all human effort and making salvation inde-pendent of man and dependent on God alone. And the dependence of salvation solely upon God makes it *ipso facto* absolutely certain, and removes it from the uncertainties and limita-tions of human action. But since even in this decision to believe there seems to be some kind of human action or contributory condition, this decision is itself referred to an immediate Divine action. In the interest of assurance of salvation the doctrine of Predestination becomes the central doctrine of Protestantism—whether with Luther, Zwingli, or Calvin, equally ori-ginal and equally necessary. Calvinism, how-ever, more and more made this doctrine the focus of its system, and in its great historical conflicts drew thence the strong support of the consciousness of election; sacrificing for this, however, rationality and universal love as elements of its conception of God; whereas, Lutheranism, in defending the two latter interests, progressively weakened down the doctrine of predestination, thereby, however, taking from its thought the heroic, the iron element. The consciously elect man feels himself to be the destined lord of the world, who in the power of God and for the honour of God has it laid on him to grasp and shape the world. The man who is simply saved by grace, also, of course, receives his salvation direct from God, but in his dread of acting on the assumptions of predestinarianism avoids any strict delimitation and relation of the spheres of God and the world, and takes refuge rather in a purely religious sphere, out of the world. The latter stands related to the religious sphere in an obscure fashion known only to God, and it is to be borne with and endured rather than dominated.

If the old interest of the certainty of salvation stands in this way in the centre, and if assurance is reached through a more inward and spiritual conception of salvation as well as by a more inward appropriation of it, it follows as a matter of course that the old fundamental idea of wholly authoritative purely Divine ordinances of salvation is retained. Along with the miracle of redemption, delivering sinners from darkness and helplessness, there continues also its correlative and continuation, the miracle of the organ of redemption, the Church. Protestantism desired to reform the Church as a whole, and was only forced against its will to set up Churches of its own. These became national Churches simply because Protestantism could only realise its ideal of the Church with the aid of governmental authority, and therefore had to be content not to apply it beyond the national frontiers. It never surrendered the thought of the Church itself as the supernatural organ of salvation, which brings

men redemption and orders their life. It
rejects only the *jus divinum* of the hierarchy
and the subordination of the civil to the
hierarchic power. The divinely appointed
preaching office and sacrament, and the
miraculous power of producing conversion
which is inherent in the word, are now the
backbone of the institution, which is left by
Luther to be freely organised, while for Calvin
it is adapted by Divine appointment to the
pattern of the primitive Church. Protestantism further rejects the idea of the sacraments
as objective healing and saving forces, to be
administered by the Church, conveying some
kind of assurance of salvation and saving
influence different from that of the word
of the Bible received by faith. It rejects
tradition, which covered the special Catholic
Church-institutions with its authority, and
holds only to the Bible, which alone is an
absolute revelation and alone possesses saving
and healing power. But it holds firmly to
the idea of the Church as the supernatural

organ of salvation, while interpreting it purely
from the Bible.   The Bible contains authoritative doctrine ; it carries with it the powers
of conversion and salvation.   It is the instru-
ment and the source of the cultus.   The
professional knowledge of it is the basis of
the sacred office.   The Bible takes the place
of the hierarchy and of the miraculous sacrament ; and the two, or three, chief sacraments
which are retained are only particular ways
of confirming one's confidence in the Bible
word—though Lutheranism in the interests of
the objectivity of the Church laid stress on
the presence of special supernatural factors
in the sacrament, to which, however, in point
of fact, no other influence was ascribed than
that belonging to the Bible word.   And,
indeed, Calvin's sacramental doctrine draws
as near as was possible, in view of the doctrine
of predestination and the general spirituality
of all saving ordinances, to this objective conception of the sacraments.

In these circumstances, the modern problem

of the relation of Church and State simply did not as yet exist. Protestantism did not see in them two distinct organisations, any more than did Catholicism; it only saw in them two distant functions in a body which is indivisibly one and the same, the *Corpus Christianum.* The applicability of religious standards to the whole body, the exclusion or, at least, disfranchisement of unbelievers and heretics, the principle of intolerance and infallibility, are for it also self-evident necessities. Luther, indeed, at first had confidence that the miraculous power of the spirit and the word would prevail alone and of themselves, but he was not able to maintain this faith against the pressure of events. Thus it was only the relation of the two functions which was readjusted. The supremacy of the hierarchy over the secular government was no longer recognised, nor was a theoretic uniformity and unity of organisation among the different national Churches. required. It is rather that both secular and civil power are alike subject to the

Bible. The civil authority serves the Church
from Christian brotherly love, regulates and
protects its position for the honour of God,
while, in the strength of their knowledge of
the word of God, the holders of the spiritual
office instruct the civil authority regarding
the demands of the Bible. A voluntary harmonious co-operation of the two functions of
the *Corpus Christianum*, and of the bearers
of these functions, is the ideal. Moreover, it
is in virtue of a Divine commission that the
civil authority undertakes the administration
of the *Lex Naturæ*, of secular and civil order,
and in this also it discharges a religious duty,
since this *Lex Naturæ* is, after all, only a part
of the perfect *Lex Naturæ* which is summed
up in the Decalogue and was recapitulated
by Christ. In virtue of this harmonious co-
operation, the spiritual authority extends its
sway over the whole range of life, including
matters of a completely secular character
which are ordered by the civil authority,
with the assistance of the divines, according

to the spirit and prescription of the Divine word. In all those essential matters which follow immediately from the Divine revelation, uniformity is indispensable. Only in the *adiaphora*,[1] *i.e.* matters not regulated by the word of God, may differences exist, though it should be said that the two Confessions held very different views as to the extent of the *adiaphora*. Only so far as they were *adiaphora* could each Confession tolerate the differences of the national Churches which it included. Things, on the other hand, which seemed to be immediately ordained by God— among the Lutherans especially sacrament and dogma; among the Calvinists also Church discipline and the eldership — must everywhere be alike or be made alike.

All this, therefore, certainly implies, as it was previously implied in Catholicism, a Church-directed civilisation; indeed here, where there was no distinction of higher and lower planes of Christian morals, it is still more strictly

[1] Lit., "things indifferent."

applied.   The idea is that of a theocracy or,
more exactly, of a " Bibliocracy."   No doubt
the form through which the theocratic government is exercised is now quite different.   It is
no longer a hierarchy issuing its commands to
the civil authority, but a " Bibliocracy " realised
by the harmonious combination of spiritual and
secular authorities.   In this root-idea the two
Confessions are entirely at one.   In its application they no doubt diverge significantly and
with important consequences.   Lutheranism
thinks, more emotionally and idealistically, of
a purely inward and spiritual working of the
Divine word.   It dispenses with any special,
detailed, independent Church-order of its own,
intended to secure the practical application of
the word of God, and with all guarantees intended to oblige the civil authority to follow
it.   Its aim is simply to place the pure word of
God on the candlestick, and it needs, in respect
of office, only a provision for the pure preaching of the word and the administration of the
sacraments.   In the realisation of this aim,

indeed, it does not recoil from the application of force; but everything else it leaves to the automatic working of the spirit which shines forth from the word. And if the secular authority refuses to submit to the word, then, submissive to the will of God, it patiently endures the cruel assaults of Satan, who is only too eager to tempt secular officials and politicians to covetousness and arrogance, or to indifference. This idealism was a marked personal characteristic of Luther, and, taking its rise from him, continued to be influential throughout the whole orthodox period, but it is also, no doubt, connected with Luther's conservative respect for authority, and with the whole of the absolutist development in the German Territories.[1] In contradistinction to

[1] [Territories, Territorialism (*v.* p. 73 *inf.*). The following quotation will serve to illustrate the use of these terms: " The Princes of the Empire present a double aspect. . . . To Charles they were collectively an oligarchy which threatened to destroy the monarchical principle embodied in the person of the Emperor; but individually, and from the point of view of their own dominions, they represented a monarchical principle similar to that which gave unity and

this, Calvinism is much more active and aggressive, but also much more systematic and politic.   It organised itself in a newly-formed republic, the very existence of which was based on Calvinism, and its spirit is dominated by the extremely systematic and rational character of Calvin, the pupil of jurists and humanists, who had never been a monk like Luther.

For all his inclusion of the Church in the general *Corpus Christianum*, and deliberate subordination, in civil matters, of the spiritual to the civil authority, he shaped a Biblical Church-order, in accordance with the demands of revelation, which made the Church more independent of the fostering Christian love of the civil authority.   He supplemented this, moreover, with a moral discipline which, in organised co-operation with the civil authority, worked out in minute detail the application of the Christian ethical standards, and in certain

strength to France, to England, and to Spain, a territorial principle more youthful and more vigorous than the effete *Kaisertum*" (A. F. Pollard in *Camb. Mod. Hist.* ii. p. 150).— TRANSLATOR.]

circumstances imposed them by force. In a case where the properly constituted authority failed to do its part, the duty devolved upon the *magistrats inférieurs*, that is to say, the official members of the community who came next in rank, to compel the erring authority to uphold the Christian standards. Calvinism, which in doctrine is more spiritualistic than Lutheranism, was in practice less spiritualistic and idealistic, and organised itself for conflict with much worldly wisdom—deriving, however, all its dispositions from the Bible ; though it must be said that for these needs it often found more appropriate counsel in the Old Testament than in the New. Thus it possessed sufficient inner strength, during the transition to the modern world and the break-up of the *Corpus Christianum*, to maintain the position of the Church, and first provisionally, and then definitively, to pass over into a free Church. Whereas, Lutheranism first fell under the sway of an unspiritual Territorialism,[1] and was

[1] See p. 71, note.

subsequently obliged to let itself be erected
by the modern State into a Church with an
elaborately complicated legal position, hover-
ing between dependence and independence.

In all this the Catholic idea of a super-
naturally directed civilisation is continued.
And still another characteristic of this civilisation survives, viz. asceticism.   No doubt it is
usual to account it a special merit of Protestantism that it made an end of asceticism and
restored secular life to an honourable status.
But it is only necessary to remember that
Protestantism retained in the strictest fashion
the determination of life by the antithesis of
heaven and hell, that by abolishing the half-
way house and postponing interval of purgatory,
it made them only more impressive than
before, that its central question regarding the
assurance of salvation is expressly concerned
with eternal deliverance from original sin.   We
have only, further, to note that Protestantism
even accentuated the Augustinian dogmas of
absolute original sin and the complete natural

corruption of all man's powers—and we shall
have to admit that the inevitable implications of
the ascetic idea have here not disappeared but
only changed their form and direction. And
that is, indeed, the fact. The change is here,
as in the case of the other alterations introduced
by Protestantism, a vast one, pregnant with
consequences, but for all that, there remains an
element which—at least in this form—is foreign
to the world of to-day, an element which
Protestantism has in common with medieval
"other-worldly" religion.

Protestantism did away with the two
different planes of Christian morality, by
means of which the old Church had effected
a compromise between the demands of secular
morality and the Early-Christian ethic, with
its indifference towards this world and direction towards the other. And it abolished
monasticism and the monastising of the
clergy. But it did not do this because it had
recognised secular goods and values as ends in
themselves in any sense whatever, but because

it saw in separation from the world an un-
allowable, because self-chosen and external,
simplification of duty. It regards the world
and its conditions as fixed at the Creation, and
as being the natural sphere and presupposition
of Christian action. From these natural presuppositions a man must not artificially with-
draw himself, and by self-created special
conditions make his task apparently more
difficult but really easier. For these only
encourage the delusion of " merit " and
human co-operation with grace, and evade
the real difficulty of the duty of possessing
the world as though one possessed it not.
There is certainly in this a stronger instinctive
valuation of the created order than Catholicism
possessed, with its idea of the supernal world and
supernal nature as supposedly more valuable
higher stages of existence, a deeper interconnexion of the natural order and the order
of redemption than Catholicism could have,
with its separation of the two and its placing
of them on different planes. Indeed, one

might say that behind this lies a different
instinctive conception of the idea of God, in
which nature and grace do not appear as
different rays of the Divine of differing
brightness, but as essentially, inherently, one.
And to this the difference between the
Catholic and Protestant doctrines of the
original condition of things bears witness.
But it applies only to the original condition.
To the condition of universal corruption
introduced by the Fall it is no longer applicable.   Since the Fall, everything—physical
world, lower creation, humanity — lies in
the night of helplessness and misery.   A
valuation of the present world for the sake
of the riches and beauty of the world, an
estimation of the goods attained in the
progress of civilisation because of an independent ethical value attaching to them, is
consequently impossible.   But precisely such
a valuation of these things is the characteristic
feature of the modern feeling towards the
world and civilisation.   The myth of the Fall

and the curse upon the world has practically ceased to have any influence in it.   And although, of course, even here a yearning for something beyond the world and civilisation makes itself keenly felt, yet the relation to nature and to the historical development of civilisation has come to be conceived in a quite different way, as one can see clearly in the ripe philosophy of Goethe's old age.   But the Reformers' recognition of the world and its civilisation is something quite different from this.   The world is for them never anything but the God-ordained sphere of our action, which we accept as we have to accept conditions of wind and weather. We have to adapt ourselves submissively thereto, and not endeavour to get away from it, but we must never set our affections on it, and never care for it for its own sake.   It is in no sense, however limited, anything Divine, but a product of God's will into which the Divine being does not itself enter.   Only for God's sake and from obedience are we to desire to have to do with it. Pain and suffering are the essence of the world, and in death and disease, misfortune and helplessness, we are constantly reminded of the curse of sin. We are to live in it and overcome it through itself, placing all our good and blessedness only in our justification and the death of Christ in our stead; we must never put our trust in the world, and must always be prepared for the punishment of sin, submitting ourselves humbly to the world and its course. Humility, obedience, trust in God, these constitute our attitude towards the world, which we accept with all its pain as the punishment of our sin, and as ordained by God, while its scanty joys are but a transient afterglow of the original goodness of the creation.

In modern literature generally, which has a particularly strong sense of the contrast in this respect, it has become customary to describe as ascetic, an ethic and outlook on the world which rest on the sharp antithesis of the

here and the hereafter and consequently treat
the present reality as an earthly vale of tears.
But originally the term " asceticism " signified
only a possible, but by no means necessary,
consequence of this view of things : systematic
practice in the renunciation and overcoming
of the world.   In the wider of these senses
the Reformation Gospel is also ascetic, in
spite of its admission of secular motives—such
motives were not, indeed, wanting in Catholicism.   This is not less asceticism because it
does not take the form of monasticism,
because it renounces the world inwardly and
from inward motives and does not outwardly
abandon it.   In contrast with Catholic asceticism, which expressed itself in a life outside
of and apart from the world, this may be
described as " intra-mundane " asceticism,[1] and

[1] The expression (*innerweltliche askese*) is coined by Max
Weber in his great work, which we shall have to estimate
more exactly at a later point, *Die protestantische Ethik und
der Geist des Kapitalismus* (" Archiv für Sozialwissenschaft
und Sozialpolitik," xx. and xxi.).   He has exhaustively
recognised the specific character of the asceticism of the
Reformed Church and the Sectaries.   The objections which

we only need to realise to ourselves the
mental atmosphere of the Renaissance, or the
glorification of the world in modern poetry,
or, again, as the sphere of modern technical
achievements, in order to feel that even this
" intra-mundane " asceticism is a real asceticism. The fact is that asceticism must necessarily follow from the premises of the whole

Loofs and Leser bring against this conception do not
appear to me conclusive. There is, after all, in Protestant
asceticism something more than a mere opposition to pure
secularism and the recognition that religion shows its
power especially amid suffering, as Loofs suggests (p. 21 f.),
and certainly something quite different from the antagonism
between creative liberty and the resisting stream of natural
tendency, as Leser thinks. Rachfahl calls attention to the
differences between Weber's conception of asceticism and
mine. But even in the present work I have clearly distinguished the Lutheran and Reformed ideas of asceticism ;
Weber is only concerned with the latter. More detail will
be found in my *Soziallehren*. The conception certainly
involves contradictions ; but the contradiction lies in the
thing which it expresses.

[As the author speaks of this expression as a new
coinage, I have ventured on the parallel formation " intra-
mundane," to indicate that the asceticism is practised
within the world and not by withdrawal from it. " Secular
asceticism " might serve, only that " secular " usually
connotes a certain temper of mind which is not here in
view.—TRANSLATOR.]

system of redemption; and a supernatural redemption from a corrupted and God-abandoned natural condition of things is also the fundamental idea of Protestantism.

So far both Confessions are at one, but in the working out of the principle they differ from one another in very important ways. The Lutheran asceticism, like other parts of the system, draws its support from Luther's idealistic spirit. It is left, without rule or compulsion, without plan or law, to the conscience of the individual. It is not rationalised and disciplined, but remains a free energy, a tone and temper of mind, and that is why in individual cases it recognises so many things as *adiaphora*. Thus it remains more free and inward. On the other hand, it also remains, in accordance with the reluctance of Lutheranism to take an active part in the world and its confidence in the automatic working of the Spirit, mainly a mere endurance and toleration of the world, which does not exclude, indeed, on occasion a thankful and obedient joy, but is nevertheless essentially a self-abnegation and submission, a transference of all hope to the blessed world of the hereafter, and a rejoicing in martyrdom in this world. This is asceticism in the wider modern sense of the word, as indicating a metaphysical attitude towards life; which, however, in a fashion characteristic of Lutheranism—and very sympathetic to human nature generally—alternates, on no principle at all, with a hearty acceptance of the good gifts of God.

Quite different is the Reformed asceticism. It is, like Calvinism as a whole, active and aggressive, desires to re-shape the world to the glory of God, and make the reprobate bow submissively to the Divine law, and will with all diligence create and maintain a Christian commonwealth. To this end it rationalises and disciplines, in its ethical theory and Church-disciplinary instruction, the whole of action. It restricts more and more closely the range of the things left by Calvin as *adiaphora* for the uses of recreation, anathematises as creature-worship every tendency to value earthly things as ends in themselves, but nevertheless demands the systematic use of all possibilities of action which are capable of contributing to the progress and well-being of the Christian commonwealth. It scorns all mere emotion and sentiment as idle and frivolous, but is inspired by a profound sense of working for the honour of God and his Church. Thus there arises, in addition to an unresting activity and strict severity, a systematic completeness and a Christian-social trend in the spirit of Calvinistic ethics. This is asceticism more in the older technical sense of the word, as a systematic disciplining of the natural man for the attainment of a goal of life which lies in the hereafter, having many points of contact with Jesuit asceticism, as has often been pointed out. Lutheranism endures the world in suffering, pain, and martyrdom, Calvinism masters it for the honour of God by untiring work, for the sake of the self-discipline which work supplies, and the well-

being of the Christian community which may
be attained by means of it. But, at bottom,
both merely applied in different ways the
asceticism inseparable from the full belief in
redemption. The Lutheran avoids "naturalism" and reliance on natural forces and impulses. The Calvinist avoids the "creature-
worship" which is involved in every form of
love of the world for its own sake. Both adapt
themselves to the wholly and immediately
Divine and "other-worldly" end to which
this world looks, but the one does so passively,
the other actively.

If all these considerations be taken into
account, it becomes obvious that Protestantism
cannot be supposed to have directly paved the
way for the modern world. On the contrary,
it appears at first, in spite of all its great new
ideas, as a revival and reinforcement of the
ideal of authoritatively imposed Church-civilisation, as a complete reaction to medieval
thinking, which sweeps away such beginnings
of a free and secular civilisation as had already

been toilsomely established.   Goethe compared it to the French Revolution: "it turned back the advance of quiet culture."   And, in addition, it supplied the incentive to a revival of the Catholic idea, and so, in spite of the contemporary diffusion of the ideas and manners of the Renaissance, Europe had to experience two centuries more of the medieval spirit.   It is true that anyone who approaches the subject from the side of political or economic history, will not receive this impression, since in these departments the movements which began in the late Middle Ages continued to develop without a break, and, indeed, to a large extent took Protestantism into their service.   But anyone who approaches it from the side of the history of religion, of social ethics or of science, will not be able to escape the impression that it was only the great struggle for freedom at the end of the seventeenth and in the eighteenth century which really brought the Middle Ages to an end.

But this only makes it a more pressing

question how, in spite of all that, Protestantism
could play a conspicuous part in the production
of the modern word.   As to the fact of its influence there can be no question. The paradox
is explained if we follow the hint which this
statement of the problem gives us,[1] and seek its
influence at first not in a universal regenera-
tion or reconstruction of life as a whole, but
mainly in indirect and unconsciously produced
effects, nay, even in accidental side-influences,
or again in influences produced against its will,
particularly if we take into account, alongside
of Protestantism proper, the effects of the
humanistic criticism which was bound up with
it, the ideal of the Baptist sectaries, and the
mystical subjectivism.   In this way it will the
more clearly appear just where the point is at
which a really direct and immediate connexion
exists.   I shall endeavour briefly to sketch
these effects in the different departments of

[1] [*I.e.,* I take it, in the use of the word "conspicuous"
(*hervorragend*)—this, the author is about to explain, it was
not, but that does not prevent its having been important.—
TRANSLATOR.]

civilisation, intentionally splitting them up under these different categories. It is only by resigning the attempt to construe everything on the basis of a single leading idea which *ex hypothesi* itself produces and shapes everything, and by taking account of the multitude of different parallel and independent—indeed, sometimes contradictory—influences, that we can arrive at an understanding of the real causal connexion. The influence of accident, that is, the combination of several independent causal series, should never be underestimated in such matters. To allow for it is not to abolish or deny the existence of the great main line of direct development of ideas, but only to protect it from confusions and disturbances. If such a development be present at all, this cautious procedure will only serve to emphasise it.

CHAPTER IV

PROTESTANTISM AND POLITICO-SOCIAL INSTITUTIONS

THE circumstance which strikes the eye first
and foremost is that Protestantism, by breaking
up the absolute autocracy of the Catholic
Church, broke the power of Church-civilisation,
in spite of its temporary revival, once and for
all.   Three infallible " Churches," unchurching
and anathematising one another, discredited
the idea of the Church, for which there is no
plural.   The sixteenth and seventeenth centuries are no longer the Middle Ages, but
neither are they " Modern Times."   They are
the " Confessional " Age of European history,
and it is only as a consequence of the mutual
attrition—by no means, it must be said, com-

plete—of these three supernatural bodies that the modern world has arisen, a world which knows, indeed, the supersensible, but not the supernatural in the medieval sense. Thus Protestantism disintegrates the Christian Church-system and its supernatural foundation, wholly against its will, but by its actual and ever more clearly apparent influence. The plurality of the Churches and their embittered struggle did more than anything else to multiply the "Libertinists and Neutralists," while in France the policy of the Chancellor L'Hôpital, and in the Netherlands that of the Orange party, and the Pacification of Ghent, tended to the same result. Special stress has rightly been laid by Richard Rothe upon the influence and significance of Protestantism in this respect.

Another point which has to be taken into account is that the inner ecclesiastical structure of the Protestant Churches, and especially of Lutheranism, is considerably weaker than that of Catholicism, and therefore when confronted with the modern world of ideas, has less

resisting power than Catholicism. That is the
point on which Paul de Lagarde has constantly
insisted with a one-sided intensity of emphasis.
Once the supreme miracle of the incarnation
of God in Jesus and in the Bible is present,
the continuation of this miracle in the hierarchy and the sacraments is a logical consequence; nothing short of the complete
deification of the Church as an Institution
can really prevent the humanisation of the
doctrines and truths. Hence, even among
the Protestant Churches, Calvinism, which
retains a remnant of the *jus divinum* in its
Church-organisation, has, down to the present
day, in England and America, offered a
stronger resistance to the disintegrating influence of modern science than have the idealistic
Church arrangements of Luther. When dis-
gust at the Confessional confusions, combined
with the development of humanistic science,
caused an attack to be made upon the Churches
generally, Protestantism was not able to maintain its previous position—has, indeed, in many

respects endeavoured to come into inner relations with the new forces, and in this way has variously and profoundly altered its inner religious character.[1]

That is, of course, only the most external and only a provisional view of the matter. The weakened powers of resistance were not responsible for everything. It is rather that Protestantism has many tendencies drawing it towards the modern world, and these enabled it, instead of simply being overwhelmed in the struggle, to amalgamate with the new element, and to amalgamate with it much more solidly than Catholicism—which did in its own fashion amalgamate with it in the civilisation of the Counter-Reformation, and in its modern development—has been able to do. I shall show this first in the different departments of civilisation, postponing to the last the most important thing, the question how far the transformation of the religious

[1] *Cf.* Rothe, *Vorlesungen über Kirchengeschichte,* edited by Weingarten, vol. ii., Heidelberg, 1875.

idea, which has taken place in Protestantism, signifies the creation of a form of religion essentially adapted to the modern world with its new aspirations.[1] The reason for this procedure is apparent from what has been said above. If we were to begin with this last point, we should be immediately plunged into the midst of the most precarious general-isations, and of all the controversial questions of modern religious thought.

Take, first, the primary element in all morality, the family. Here Protestantism abolished the monastic and clerical view of the conjugal relation, encouraged the increase of population, so important for the rise of the modern State, created in its pastorate a new social order and a pattern of family life as Protestantism understood it. By abolish-ing the sacramental character of the married state, it put marriage on the basis of a more

[1] *Cf.* the extraordinarily suggestive investigations of Dilthey in the *Archiv für Geschichte der Philosophie,* iv. 1891 ; v. 1892 ; vi. 1893.

ethical and personal relation, made possible
divorce and remarriage, and thus prepared
the way for a freer movement of the individual. The ideal of virginity entirely
disappears from religion and ethics. Marriage
and the family, on the other hand, are the
highest and most specialised form of love to
one's neighbour, the germ-cell of all industry,
the archetype of human sociological relations,
the primal form of the Church, the most
general state, ordained by God in Paradise,
into which it is everyone's duty to enter. It
provides, in conjunction with public order
and property, the conditions established by the
Law of Nature under which Christian love
is to display itself. But all the same, in
respect to the ideal of the family itself, the
distinction from Catholicism and the approxi-
mation to modern ways of thinking are less
marked than is often supposed. Protestantism retained the old patriarchalism with the
complete subordination of the wife and
children, and its doctrine of original sin affixed

to the sexual relation sin's penalty of concupis-
cence, and to procreation the stigma of perpetuating original sin, exactly like the old
doctrine. Marriage remains for it also mainly
a prophylactic against the sinful depravity of
lust, and is accepted by Christian obedience as
a state and vocation which has now, at any
rate, been ordained by God. Calvinism, in
accordance with its rational spirit, placed in
the foreground its purpose in the begetting
and bringing up of children, and by that very
fact made the sexual emotions purely a means
to an end—if it did not entirely exclude them.
In either case, however, there is a strong
contrast with the modern development of
the family ideal and of sexual ethics. The
modern individualism, the humanity and
freedom of education, the independence of
woman, are lacking—indeed, the abolition of
the cloister still further discredited the position
of the unmarried woman as compared with
the married. In contrast with that stands
a spiritual and social independence of woman

among the humanists and in the Renaissance, the religious emancipation of woman among the Anabaptists, Independents, Quakers, and Pietists ; while in the education of children it was Rousseau and Pestalozzi who first struck out new paths.   Then, too, the emotional refinement of the sexual relation and the complete severance of sexual feeling from the thought of original sin have only been effected by modern art and poetry, above all by the poetry of sentiment, which is nothing else than the secularisation of the intense religious emotions and the direction of them towards natural interests.[1]   On the other hand, the dangers of over-population, the rendering difficult of the family life by economic causes, the problem of celibacy imposed by social

[1] *Cf.* my *Soziallehren.*   For late medieval family and social ethics we may here give a further reference to R. Köbner, "Die Eheanschauung des ausgehenden Mittelalters," in the *Archiv für Kulturgeschichte,* ix. 1911. On the transformation of the life of religious emotion into sentimental eroticism, see the very interesting explanations in von Waldberg's *Der empfindsame Roman in Frankreich,* 1906.

conditions, the sexual problem in relation to the vast masses of population in the big towns, and many others, are still remote from early Protestantism. It was not called on to give an answer to many questions which now imperatively demand one. It recommended early marriage, and regarded the light-hearted begetting of children as a proof of belief in Providence, a numerous progeny as a blessing from God. That is a healthy and courageous view of the matter, agreeing, moreover, with that of Jewish and Catholic ethics. But everyone knows that in modern conditions of life these matters are much more complicated.

Another element of fundamental importance consists in the legal relations of society. Here, too, Protestantism has not been without influence. It is true that in the department of criminal law it carried on the traditions of the old barbaric justice, and further, on its own part, based it on the thought of original sin and of the civil authority as the representative of the retributive justice of God. Vengeance and

7

retribution in the name of God by the civil
authority which is charged therewith, whose
function in relation to sinners is in fact that
of "the sword": such is the character of this
justice.[1] With the prevailing conception of
the *Lex Naturæ* as creating the earthly
authorities in the natural course of things
under the direction of the Divine providence,
and as receiving its particular form in view of
the duty of repressing original sin, they could
also regard this criminal law as derived from
the *Lex Naturæ*, and confirm this from Biblical
examples of the working of the *Lex Naturæ*,
which is itself expressly testified to in the Old
Testament.[2] That trial for witchcraft and
sorcery continued is a familiar fact. The
humanisation of punitive justice and the
abolition of trial for witchcraft are, as is well
known, the work of the period of Illuminism.
The punishment of witchcraft was opposed only
by isolated mystics and spiritualists.

[1] Gierke, *Genossenschaftsrecht*, iii. 713 ff. and 799 ff.
[2] [*Cf.* p. 111 f. below for the illustration of this.—TRANSLATOR.]

In Civil Law, also, it is impossible to speak
of any kind of innovations of principle.
Luther himself, under the impression of the
Sermon on the Mount, had scruples about the
Christianity of law in general, and looked on
it as only a concession to the conditions of the
present sinful state ; but for that he demanded,
with simple peasant shrewdness, at least popular
and equitable laws.   Calvin, a jurist and man
of the world by early training, was not inspired
with any scruples on this head by the Sermon
on the Mount, but, on the contrary, regarded
a good and well-developed legal system as
one of the chief instruments of a sound social
order, such as should conduce to the realisation
of the ends of the Christian life.   Only an
indirect significance is here to be ascribed to
the Reformation, in so far, namely, as it contributed to the adoption of Roman Law.   That,
it is true, was more due to the influence of the
Protestant humanists than of the Protestant
spirit, which has nothing to do with Roman
Law as such.   The Protestant humanists, how-

ever, construed the *Lex Naturæ* as the basis of the whole of the natural life, as the order which under the Divine providence issues from reason and the course of things, and identified the *Lex Naturæ*, again, with the Decalogue. But since they also, with a truly humanistic valuation of antiquity, and following hints given by the Roman jurists, regarded the Roman Law as the law of reason and *ratio scripta*, it became for them an expression of the *Lex Naturæ* and hence a development of the Decalogue. Melanchthon went so far as to identify Roman Law with the Decalogue, as did also the Genevan theologians, whose chief ambition it was to have alongside of the theological faculty a juristic faculty formed of pupils of the great French school of Jurisprudence. In Germany the needs of the Territorial State and of Absolutism, in Calvinistic countries economic conditions, supported this theologico-humanistic theory. The learned professional judiciary eagerly used these formulas in support of its influence and

position. All this, of course, does not apply
to Anglo-Saxon countries, where the adoption
of the Roman Law did not take place.[1]

If a general transformation of civilisation
necessarily finds expression in a change of legal
theory and in new legal forms given to the
practical relations of life, then Protestantism
is no new civilisation. In essentials it continued the medieval conditions, and, where it
allowed itself to be influenced by changes proceeding from general circumstances, that was
a learned application, but not the direct action,
of its spirit. In contrast with this, both the
medieval and the modern world have produced
for themselves a system of law and a distinctive
legal consciousness—a clear indication that the
Confessional Protestantism of the sixteenth
and seventeenth centuries was not a new and
distinctive principle of civilisation. The "Law
of Nature" movement, with which the modern
legal development begins, is not, particularly

---

[1] *Cf.* Troeltsch, *Melanchthon und Joh. Gerhard,* 1891.
Also my *Soziallehren.*

in the departments of criminal and civil law, an offspring of the spirit of Protestantism.

On the other hand, it did, of course, introduce important innovations in the domain of Church Law. It was not merely that Luther cast off the Canon Law; the whole spirit of the Reformation is directly opposed to the idea of a divinely established ecclesiastical legal Institution with a world-ruling and world-embracing organisation. But here, too, things are extraordinarily complicated. A new form of law for the newly-arisen religious society was not, in truth, discovered by Lutheranism. After all kinds of confusions, it finally had recourse to the Canon Law again, and, striking out what was specifically Catholic, adapted it to Protestant circumstances; a solution of the question which, after the Inter-Confessionalising of the States, was no longer tenable, but which, with all its illogicalities and inconsistencies, continues to the present day. Calvinism created for itself, in the framework of its church-session, "classis" [presbytery], and synod, an organisation inspired by its own spirit, and, by appealing to its Divine institution in the Bible, gave it a victorious strength. But this organisation also was dependent, on one side, on the Confessional unity of the State and an indissoluble union of the interests of State and Church. On another side it is dependent on the exclusion of any conception of the Bible as human and historically developed; and with its *jus divinum* it contradicted the genuine Protestant spirit. Consequently, its Church Law also, since the period of Illumination and the break-up of the Confessional State, has fallen into desuetude. Outwardly it has in the main become independent of the State, and inwardly it has for the most part given up the *jus divinum*. The main thing is that neither Confession has been able to solve the problem of Protestant organisation, the reconciliation of the free inwardness, regulated by conscience, of individual religious conviction with the requirements of a Society based on a common cultus and

administration.   In this respect they reverted
completely to the analogy of Catholicism, the
compulsory maintenance of orthodox Church
doctrine, and revived prosecution for heresy.
Indeed, as it was now belief and not cultus
which stood in the centre, the compulsory
imposition of doctrine was stricter, more
universal, and more pedantically exact than
in Catholicism.   If the general tendency of
modern Protestantism is in the direction of a
Free-Church system loosed from the State,
and if it seeks to provide within the Church
room for freedom of movement and the
constant communication of life by the Spirit,
these aims are not derived from the great
Confessions, but partly from the Anabaptist
movement, which was not without influence
in the turning of Calvinism towards Free
Churchism, partly from the Spiritualistic
Mysticism, which stood for the free and
unmediated action of the Spirit.   But these
tasks awaiting a new organisation of Protestant
religious life have scarcely been recognised

and formulated down to the present day, and are infinitely difficult to discharge, difficult especially because we have here everywhere to contend with the remnants of Catholicising Church Law, which, on its part, has its basis in very familiar and influential characteristics of average humanity.   But if Protestantism had really been so clear and comprehensive a new principle of thought and action as is often asserted, then the most difficult problem of civilisation, the delimitation of the spheres of the religious and secular societies, and the defining of the relations of the religious society towards individual freedom of belief, would long ago have been much more energetically, courageously, and successfully taken in hand.

Naturally, with this alteration of Church Law went a similar alteration in the domain of politics and Public Law,[1] and this change became

[1] [" The term Public Law," writes T. E. Holland, "which is in daily use in the legal speculation and practice of the continent of Europe, unfortunately finds no equivalent in our insular legal terminology.   An English lawyer, when

of really high significance for the development
of the modern State. But here, too, we
must guard against current exaggerations; the
secular State and the modern idea of the State,
and an independent political ethic, are not
creations of Protestantism. What is true is
that it freed the State from all and every kind
of subordination to the hierarchy; it taught
men to regard civil callings as direct service of
God and not as indirect service through the
intermediary of the Church. That signifies
the final—both formal and theoretical—independence of the State. But it nevertheless is
not yet equivalent to the modern idea of the
State. So far from that, Protestantism regarded the State as a religious institution, and
saw its end and aim in the protection of the
Christian commonwealth and the moral law.
Since the proper end of life lies only in

he had been made to understand the idea, would probably
come to the conclusion that it covers . . . Constitutional
law, Ecclesiastical law, Revenue law, and Pleas of the
Crown" (*Elements of Jurisprudence*, ed. 2, cap. xvi.
p. 273).—TRANSLATOR.]

redemption and the religious ethic, there
remains for the State only the character of
protector of the *disciplina externa* and of
justitia civilis, together with the practical care
of the material existence of its subjects; in
performing these duties it is only discharging
the functions of the *Lex Naturæ*, which is
summed up in the Decalogue. Beyond main-
taining these external pre-conditions of the
Christian life, its highest office is the loving
service of the Church, whereto the civil
authority is bound, both by the Law of Nature
as the protector of the embodiment of the
Law of Nature in the Decalogue, and by
Christian principle as the most important
member of the Christian community. The
Protestant theory of the State is in both
Confessions based on that very same Christian
" Law of Nature " which, in the Middle Ages,
was compounded out of Stoicism, Aristotle,
and the Bible, and which Protestants continued
carefully to build up with a view to their
biblico-rational conception of the State. The

only difference is that the authority now does
all this from an independent understanding of
the Biblico-rational demand, in virtue of its
own divinely ordained commission, and in a
wholly free co-operation with the professional
experts in Biblical knowledge, the bearers of
the spiritual office.   Of course, that implies an
advance in the autonomy and independence
of the idea of the State, and a step forward
towards the secularisation of the State, the
recognition of a natural ethical worth properly
belonging to it, and needing no ecclesiastical
sanction.   The principles which Machiavelli
and Bodin developed, in opposition to the
Christian consciousness, here become capable of
combining with it and being strengthened by
it.   Protestantism intervened in the development of the State in the direction of autonomy,
and powerfully furthered it.   In particular, it
invested the expanding civil officialdom with
the character of a God-ordained calling, which
plays its part in the execution of the Divine
will; and it thus gave to the new centralised

administration a strong ethical reinforcement.
Then, too, by directly inciting the State to
work for the advancement of civilisation,
spiritual and material, in the interests of the
Christian commonwealth, it inspired the civil
government to set before it the widest civilising aims, and put into its hands the care of
education, moral order, oversight of food
supply, and spiritual and ethical well-being.
This is not quite the modern idea of the State
as the organ of civilisation, for all this is done
by the State in its joint exercise of spiritual
authority and in the discharge of Christian
duty.   But out of it, by the separation of
civilisation from the Church, while the civilising functions are retained by the State, there
arises the modern idea of the State as the
organ of civilisation.   Enlightened "minor's
guardian" absolutism, after the Prussian style,
grows out of the Protestant patriarchalism.
The latter, indeed, was met with chiefly on
the soil of Lutheranism, which directly assigned
Church functions to the State; Calvinism

distinguished the Church's care of spiritual interests and general welfare more sharply from that of the State, and from the first, in Geneva, kept the Academy under Church supervision. Nevertheless, it also—at least where the Genevan ideal prevailed—gave the State a direct and generous share in the work of spiritual and ethical elevation and the pursuit of the ideals of civilisation. Of course, as soon as the State refused these duties in their spiritual aspect, Calvinism took them back into the hands of the Church, leaving the State in the main only the rôle of a guardian responsible for safety and discipline, thus preparing the way for the idea of the State held by the earlier Liberalism. In America, the Churches themselves to this day maintain this purely utilitarian idea of the State; and the Dutch theological Minister, Kuyper, actually made it a fundamental principle of the Reformed Church.

In all this, Protestantism is only strengthening impulses which were already present. Of

a more marked character was its influence on
the State in regard to form and constitution.
That applies, however, in the main, only to
Calvinism.   In this point the two Confessions
differ fundamentally.   Everything depends
here upon the form given, in the one case and
the other, to the Law of Nature as adopted in
the Churches, just as that had been the decisive
factor   previously   in   the   Catholic   system.
Lutheranism, in its conception of the Law of
Nature, is thoroughly conservative ; and in its
complete confidence in God's providence it
regards the powers called into being in the
natural course of things as *ipso facto* instituted
by God and commissioned to be the protectors
of the *justitia civilis*.   The   Old   Testament,
moreover, supported this theory, by repre-
senting Saul and David as appointed by God.
God is the *causa remota* of the constituted
authorities, and consequently men owe them,
as powers whose authority is directly or indirectly derived from God, an unconditional
obedience.   In   virtue   of   this   conception

Lutheranism facilitated the transition from the State-authority of the privileged orders to a Territorial absolutism; and by putting Church authority also into its hands, immensely increased the resources of this absolutism. Nevertheless, it preserves the spirit of the orders, since, while it requires of them subordination to the central authority, it also, on the other hand, accords to them, within their jurisdiction, a similar status as God-ordained authorities, and recognises their claim to passive obedience.   Lutheranism is thus far politically favourable to absolutism, but, on the whole, is essentially conservative and politically neutral; it destroys the powers of the orders in the upward direction, but preserves them in the downward.   The doctrines of Stahl and the Prussian conservatism still express its spirit; only, it must not be forgotten that in the older Lutheranism "By the grace of God" applied not only to the sovereign but also to the magistracy of the Imperial cities, and represents simply a religious interpretation of natural events, unconnected with feudal romanticism.[1]

Quite different was the development of the political spirit of Calvinism. Generally speaking, its State-adaptation of the Law of Nature is at bottom also conservative, though where it has open to it the possibility of the free choice and constitution of new authorities, it prefers a modified aristocracy, as is not surprising in view of its original connexion with the Genevan republic, and the prominence which it gives to the aristocratic idea of predestination. But in its great struggles with the Catholic governments which proscribed the pure word of God, that is to say, the Huguenot, Netherlandish, Scottish, and English struggles, Calvinism gave a much more radical development to its Law of Nature. It successfully established the principle of the right of resist-

[1] *Cf.* P. Drews, *Einfluss der gesellschaftlichen Zustände auf das kirchliche Leben,* Tübingen, 1906, and the same writer's *Der evangelische Geistliche in der deutschen Vergangenheit,* Jena, 1906; (Gebhardt) *Zur bäuerlichen Glaubens- und Sittenlehre,* Gotha, 1895.

8

ance, which must be exercised on behalf of the
word of God in the face of ungodly authorities,
the exercise of which becomes the duty of the
magistrats inférieurs as the next in order as
holders of the Divine commission, while, fail-
ing these, it must be put in practice even by
the individual; indeed, in virtue of a special
individual call thereto, the assassination of
a tyrant is permissible, as in the case of Jael
and Sisera.

This more radical conception gives to the
Calvinistic Law of Nature a tendency towards
progress, an impulse to reorganise governmental
conditions when these were of an " ungodly "
character.   Moreover, in these attempts at
reorganisation themselves, there appears a
specifically Reformed idea of the State.   For
in all such reorganisations the germ-cell was
the   Reformed   presbyterial   and   synodical
Church-order, with its representative system.
Thus, in the natural course of things, this
system tended towards the theory that the
State ought to be reorganised — the State

itself must be built up on representative lines
and ruled by a *collegium* consisting of those
put forward as the " best " by the choice of
the electors.   Under the influence of these
ideas, as has been pointed out especially by
Gierke, the Calvinistic conception of the Law
of Nature took up into itself the idea of
the State-contract.   On these lines the *Lex
Naturæ* leads by the logic of events to a
constitution and choice of authorities based
on contract.   These can then, as deriving
their status from God as the *causa remota*, be
regarded in a wholly religious aspect as God-
appointed, and can lay claim to absolute obedience so long as they do not offend against the
word of God.   The Old Testament confirmation of this doctrine of the Law of Nature,
which Calvinism characteristically seeks in a
different direction from Lutheranism, is found
in Israel's covenants, from which its kings
and its ordinances are derived.   Hence the
Protestant " Covenants."   This is still, however, an essentially religious and aristocratic

idea, sharply distinguished from the pure
rationalism of the conception of the Law
of Nature in the period of Illuminism, and
from the democratic sympathies of Rousseau's
teaching.   In every case where the theory
has come to practical application, it has led
to an aristocracy based on a limited franchise.
Democracy in the strict sense is everywhere
foreign to the Calvinistic spirit, and could
only develop out of it where, as in the New
England States, the old class-system of Europe
was absent and political institutions grew
directly out of those of the Church.   But
there, too, it developed into the strictest theocracy.   It required as a condition of eligibility
to office, Church-membership voluntarily pro-
fessed, subsequently to baptism, combined
with moral worth, while the chosen rulers
regarded themselves as having the right to
exercise in patriarchal fashion the strictest
ethico-religious discipline.   The democratis-
ing of the modern world ought not, therefore,
to be solely and directly referred to Calvinism.

The Rationalism which, wholly dissociated from religious considerations, appealed to the pure Law of Nature, has in this connexion a much stronger significance; but all the same, Calvinism took a prominent part in preparing the way for the upgrowth of the democratic spirit.[1]

Another fundamental idea of modern political life is that of the " rights of man " and freedom of conscience. That is to say, the theoretical inviolability of the life, freedom, and property of the individual apart from regular process of law, and the respecting of the individual's religious beliefs and expressed convictions. These rights have passed from the French constitution into all other modern constitutions, and are therefore everywhere bound up with the ideas of democracy and representative government. But for the understanding of these rights of the individual,

[1] *Cf.* on this Gierke, *Althusius*, ed. 2, Breslau, 1902; Cardauns, *Lehre vom Widerstandsrecht des Volkes im Luthertum und Kalvinismus,* Bonn, 1903 ; Doyle, *The English in America,* London, 1887.

and especially for our present inquiry, it is
of importance that these two, the rights of
man and democracy, are not simply coincident,
and are therefore not to be explained by the
historical derivation of one from the other.
It is quite possible for the rights of the individual to exist apart from democracy, under
any form of government which recognises and
protects them, just as, conversely, there can be
a democracy in which terrorism and fanatical
zeal for equality, or, again, dogmatic prejudice,
preclude freedom of conscience.   The English
constitutional monarchy of the " Glorious Revolution " practically recognised the rights of
the individual and liberty of conscience, without democracy, while the Calvinistic New
England States, and, for that matter, Rousseau's
majority-rule, had democracy without liberty
of conscience.   The two ideas have to be kept
separate, and only coalesce where the democratic shaping of the ideas of the State is held to
be itself an inalienable human right; which,
however, neither is nor was by any means a

logical necessity. It is the old and well-known antithesis between freedom and equality, which in general differentiates the Anglo-Saxon from the Latin conception of Society. Attention has been called to this point by Jellinek, who also showed that in the French constitution these two elements are separate and strongly distinguished. But then the question arises: Whence comes the idea of the rights of the individual? Following out this question, Jellinek shows that it is derived from the Constitutions of the North American States, and in part verbally taken over from them. And in the North American States themselves he derived these declarations from their Puritan religious principles, which, not content with the old practical character of English liberties, regarded the freedom of the person, and especially of religious conviction, as a right conferred absolutely by God and Nature, which is essentially inviolable by any State. It was only in virtue of being thus put on a religious basis that these demands became

absolute, and consequently admitted of and
required a theoretic legal exposition. It was
thus that they first passed into Constitutional
Law as a fundamental doctrine, finding their way
from the North American State-constitutions
into the French, and thence into almost all
modern constitutions. What the purely practical English Law, utilitarian and sceptical toleration, and abstract literary theorising, had either
not felt to be necessary, or not succeeded in
securing, was now secured by the energy of a
principle based on religious conviction. It was
due to the circumstances of the time that the
penetration into the legal code of this demand
for religious freedom carried along with it the
democratic constitutional-law guarantees which
had been formulated with a view to confirming
the fundamental claim, and in conformity with
the special character of Anglo-American life ;
so that the official list of the " rights of man "
contains, besides, a series of democratic political
claims. In the latter, moreover, the influence
of the literature of European Illuminism is

unmistakable. If all this is correct, we should
certainly be in presence of an extremely important influence of Protestantism, for it must
be held to have introduced into practical
politics a fundamental law and a fundamental
ideal of modern existence, and secured its
general acceptance as a legal principle. The
fact is that Jellinek's treatment of the subject
represents, on the whole, a really illuminating
discovery, but there is just one point in which
it needs closer definition, and that point is
of decisive importance for our inquiry. That
is in respect to the Puritanism which he
asserts to have been the parent of this idea
and the creator of these legal formulæ. For
this Puritanism is not Calvinistic, but is a
sublimated essence of " Free-Church " Anabaptist and Spiritualistic-subjectivist ideas, in
combination with the old Calvinistic idea of the
inviolability of the Divine Majesty, the former
being essentially connected with the transition
to a rationalistic mode of basing these claims.
The Calvinistic Puritan States of North

America were, it is true, democratic, but, so
far from recognising liberty of conscience, they
explicitly rejected it as implying a godless
scepticism.   Liberty of conscience obtained
only in Rhode Island, and this State was
Baptist, and was therefore hated by all the
neighbour States as a hotbed of anarchy.   Its
great organiser, Roger Williams, actually went
over to Baptist beliefs, and thence passed to
an undogmatic Spiritualism.   And the second
home of liberty of conscience in North America,
the Quaker State of Pennsylvania, was also
of Baptist and Spiritualist origin.   In other
places where the claim to toleration and liberty
of conscience is found, it has political and
utilitarian motives—in the end, indeed, the
merchants of the Massachusetts theocracy
yielded to this indifferentism.   The parent
of the "rights of man" was therefore not
actual Church Protestantism, but the Sectarianism and Spiritualism which it hated and
drove forth into the New World.   And this
can surprise no one who understands the

inner structure of orthodox Protestant, and of Baptist and Spiritualist, thought.[1]

But at this point, now that our attention has been directed to these groups, there opens out before us a much wider range of vision. The North American Baptist and Quaker movements are derived from the great religious movement of the English Revolution, viz. Independency. This Independency was itself most strongly interpenetrated with Baptist influences, which, arising from the remnants of the earlier English Anabaptists, from Holland—the Continental asylum of the Anabaptists—and from the American refugees, reacted upon England. Not less strongly did

[1] *Cf.* Jellinek, *System der subjektiven öffentlichen Rechte*, ed. 2, 1905, and the same author's *Die Erklärung der Bürgerrechte*, ed. 2, Leipzig, 1904 ; Doyle, *The English in America* ; L. W. Bacon, *A History of American Christianity*, New York, 1897. References to the importance of the rationalistic literature in Wahl, "Zur Geschichte der Menschenrechte," in *Hist. Zeitschrift*, ciii., and Hägermann, "Die Erklärungen der Menschenrechte," in Ebering's *Historische Studien* for 1910. The latter, it should be said, shows very little acquaintance with the religious world of ideas.

the mystical Spiritualism exercise an influence tending to disintegrate ecclesiastical systems and to strengthen the demand for liberty of conscience.   It was now at last the turn of the step-children of the Reformation to have their great hour in the history of the world. Baptist Free-Churchism, democratic and communistic ideas, Spiritualistic non-Churchism, Pietistic Calvinism with a radical bent—all these tendencies entered into alliance with the consequences of the political catastrophe and the implications of earlier English Law.   From this coalition arose, urged on by the army of the Saints, the demand for a Christian State, which should leave the form of the worship of God free to the different independent congregations, while securing Christian morality by strict regulations, and employing the civil power in the service of the Christian cause. The Cromwellian Commonwealth, which was avowedly intended to be a Christian State, for a short time realised this idea ; and short as was the time during which this grandiose edifice lasted, its influence on the history of the world was extraordinarily great. For as a legacy from this momentous episode there remained the great ideas of the separation of Church and State, toleration of different Church societies alongside of one another, the principle of Voluntaryism in the formation of these Church-bodies, the (at first, no doubt, only relative) liberty of conviction and opinion in all matters of world-view and religion. Here. are the roots of the old liberal theory of the inviolability of the inner personal life by the State, which was subsequently extended to more outward things ; here is brought about the end of the medieval idea of civilisation, and coercive Church-and-State civilisation gives place to individual civilisation free from Church direction. The idea is at first religious. Later, it becomes secularised, and overgrown by the rationalistic, sceptical, and utilitarian idea of toleration. On the Continent it received a purely rationalistic and Illuminist under-pinning. But its real foundations were

laid in the English Puritan Revolution. The
momentum of its religious impulse opened the
way for modern freedom.   But this is not,
properly speaking, the work of Protestantism,
but of the revived Baptist and Spiritualist
movements, in combination with Calvinism of
a radical tendency.   The former now received
a belated compensation for the immense
sufferings which the religion of toleration and
respect for conscientious conviction had had
to undergo at the hands of all the Confessions
in the sixteenth century.[1]

Further political consequences, beyond those
now enumerated, are hardly to be ascribed to
Protestantism.   The break-up of the Catholic
Romano-Germanic Empire, and the transformation of Western Christendom into a
system of equipoise between the Great Powers,
was, of course, facilitated and confirmed by

---

[1] On this see Weingarten, *Revolutionskirchen Englands,*
1868; Gooch, *History of English Democratic Ideas,* 1898; and
my *Soziallehren.*   The criticisms of Loofs, p. 15, are to some
extent justified; I had previously followed Weingarten
too closely.

it; but the process was already in progress before Protestantism arose. With the principle of nationality its system of national Churches has no connexion whatever. This contributed, no doubt, to the concentration of power in the hands of the central authorities, but the principle of nationality was the product of two completely modern, though in some respects, contrasted forces—the democratic awakening of the masses and the Romantic idea of the National Spirit.

CHAPTER V

Protestantism and Economic Organisation, Social Developments, Science and Art

When we turn, however, to the development of economic life and thought, we again become aware of a powerful influence. Here Laveleye long since pointed to a fundamental significance of Protestantism, and in the references frequently made at the present day to the "backwardness of the Catholic populations" the same idea is expressed. But here, too, things are far from being quite simple; and many errors are in circulation. Thus, for example, people are fond of praising Luther's ethic of the secular calling, and seeing in it the Christian justification of industrial life,

which is supposed to have taken a great leap
forward in consequence of this justification.
But to do this is to forget that the doctrine
of the " calling," as a doctrine of the systematic
contribution of every worker to the *de lege
naturæ* appointed purpose of Society, had
already long been a doctrine of Catholicism,
and that the only difference was that for
Luther the monastic and ascetic limitations
disappeared, and the secularisation of Church
property increased the wealth and power of
the Territorial sovereigns, and thus facilitated
the adoption by the governments of a rational
economic policy. And another point which
is forgotten is that the Protestant theory of
the calling, as held by Lutheranism, was
closely bound up with a conservative Society
organised on a class-system, and tended to
keep each individual in his own class ; it only
demanded the securing of the necessaries of
existence and the protection of food-supply
by the civil authority ; apart from this, it
requires the patient endurance of the injustices

9

of the world. This is the same traditional
attitude towards life as was prescribed by
Catholicism, and was as far as possible from
giving an initial impetus to the mighty
upward movement of modern economic life.
In complete accordance with this, Luther's
economic ideal is conceived wholly from the
point of view of agriculture and handicrafts,
and he takes for granted the Canon-law prohibition of interest.   Indeed, he attacks
finance and credit, and in particular whole-
sale trade, as passionately as any medieval
author.   This attitude could not, of course,
be completely maintained in practice, and
the theological ethic of his successors before
long softened down his prescriptions.   But
Lutheran religion never contained an impulse
towards a vigorous economic development,
and in view of the subsequent decline of
German prosperity, it never had a chance to
develop such an impulse.   The economic
results of Lutheranism were, therefore, confined to the strengthening of the national

government, and, and, as an indirect consequence, of " Mercantilism," [1] and to the education of a humble and patient working class, fitted to the needs of the manorial estate, which still at the beginning of the nineteenth century furnished the sweeping advance of industrialism and capitalism with a docile labour supply. The actually existing more advanced economic development of the Protestant portion of the population in Germany must have had, in the first instance, other than religious grounds, and can only have been indirectly supported by the qualities of activity, industry, and frugality inculculated by the Lutheran ethic, or by the growing consciousness of individuality, and the increasing zeal for popular education.

A much greater importance in this respect must be attributed to Calvinism. Here, as

[1] [The reference here is doubtless to the earlier form of " Mercantilism," in which it aimed at fostering a self-contained " home " trade, rather than to the later form, in which it encouraged exports and discouraged imports.— TRANSLATOR.]

in politics, it is the power which stands nearer to the modern world. It has, indeed, always been emphasised that Calvin and his successors rejected the Canon-law prohibition of interest, and did away with the burdensome restrictions on investment; that Geneva, with the support of the *Vénérable Compagnie*,[1] established a bank and introduced industries; that the Calvinistic countries and settlements everywhere show the expansion of industrialism and capitalism. This, however, is not a complete account of the matter. The real significance of Calvinism for the modern economic development which culminates in the all-embracing capitalistic system of the present day lies much deeper. It has lately been pointed out by Max Weber, who, in the course of his investigation of the great main problem of present-day economic history, the problem of the character and origin of capitalism, raised the question regarding the spiritual, ethical, and philosophical pre-suppositions of

[1] [The council of ministers and teachers.—TRANSLATOR.]

this system. Without a definite mental and spiritual background, a system of this kind cannot become dominant, or as Sombart, in dealing with a similar problem, has expressed it: In the minds of the mass of its supporters, or at least in those of its founders, apart from the external occasions, inducements, and incentives, there must be a basis of definite economic attitude. From the capitalistic system we have to distinguish the "capitalistic spirit," apart from which the former would never have come to exercise such power over men's minds. For this spirit displays an untiring activity, a boundlessness of grasp, quite contrary to the natural impulse to enjoyment and ease, and contentment with the mere necessaries of existence; it makes work and gain an end in themselves, and makes men the slaves of work for work's sake; it brings the whole of life and action within the sphere of an absolutely rationalised and systematic calculation, combines all means to its end, uses every minute to the full, employs

every kind of force, and in alliance with
scientific technology and the calculus which
unites all these things together, gives to life
a clear calculability and abstract exactness.
This spirit, Weber said to himself, cannot
have simply arisen of itself as a necessary con-
comitant of industrial inventions, discoveries,
and commercial gains. For it did not arise
with the banking business of the late Middle
Ages, with the capitalism of the Renaissance,
or the Spanish colonisation—here it had to
struggle with an opposing spirit, the conscience
as educated by Catholicism, and was forced
to strike a compromise. Following this line
of thought, Weber was led, by way of con-
jecture from the fact that capitalism flourishes
best on Calvinistic soil, to draw the conclusion
that the ethico-religious spirit of Calvinism
had a special significance for the arising of
this capitalistic spirit. By means of a detailed
investigation he showed that it was the Calvinistic asceticism which produced on a large
scale, not so much capitalism as the capitalistic

spirit on which it was based, and thus created
the psychological conditions in which the
vast expansion of a system at bottom so
contrary to nature as capitalism, could come
into being and establish itself firmly—which
does not, of course, hinder the fact that capitalism extends its influence over men to whom
Calvinism means nothing.   Of course, the
operation of other mental and spiritual influences is not excluded.   Among these
Weber himself especially named Judaism;
and Sombart has gone on to assert a close
spiritual affinity between the Jewish and
the Calvinistic economic attitude, and has
explained it by the well-known fact that
Calvinism made use of the Jewish ethical
teaching.   The latter explanation, in my
opinion, while not altogether without foundation, does not sufficiently take account of
the limited and complex character of the
relation.   When all is said and done, Calvinism remains the real nursing-father of the
civic, industrial capitalism of the middle

classes.   Self - devotion to work and gain,
which constitutes the involuntary and unconscious asceticism of the modern man, is
the child of a conscious "intra-mundane"[1]
asceticism of work and calling inspired by
religious motives.   The "spirit of the calling,"
which does not reach out beyond the world
but works in the world without "creature-
worship," that is, without love of the world,
becomes the parent of a tireless systematic-
ally disciplined laboriousness, in which work
is sought for work's sake, for the sake of the
mortification of the flesh, in which the produce
of the work serves, not to be consumed in enjoyment, but to the constant reproduction of
the capital employed.   Since the aggressively
active ethic inspired by the doctrine of predestination urges the elect to the full development of his God-given powers, and offers him
this as a sign by which he may assure himself of his election, work becomes rational
and systematic.   In breaking down the motive

[1] See p. 80, footnote.

of ease and enjoyment, asceticism lays the
foundations of the tyranny of work over
men. And from the fact that the produce
of this work is in no way an end in itself,
but advances the general well-being, and that
all return which goes beyond an adequate
provision for the needs of life is felt to be
merely a stimulus to the further employment
and increase of it, there results the principle
of the illimitability and infinitude of work.
On the basis of this economic attitude there
arose the early capitalism of the Huguenots, of
Holland, England, and America ; and even to
the present day in America and Scotland, as
well as among the English Nonconformists, the
higher capitalism is clearly seen to be closely
connected with it.   A similar development has
taken place among the Pietistic groups, which
were to a great extent allied to and influenced
by Calvinism in this religious ascetic idea ; and
also among the Baptist communities, which
abandoned Communism in favour of the Protestant "ethic of the calling," for they all, find-

ing themselves excluded from public life, turned
to economic activities, and tabooing the aim of
enjoyment, declared production for production's
sake to be a commandment of religion.

Weber has, in my opinion, completely
proved his case; though perhaps it ought to
be more strongly emphasised that the special
character of the Reformed asceticism was
partly determined by the special conditions
of the commercial situation in the western
countries, and more especially by the
exclusion of Dissent from political life, with
its opportunities and responsibilities, just as,
on the other hand, the traditional Lutheran
view became emphasised during the economic
decline of Germany.   How far, in detail, the
particular developments, as well as the general
fact of the capitalistic system, have grown out
of the capitalistic spirit of Calvinism, and
what other forces have had a share in producing and strengthening it, need not here be
made the subject of further inquiry.   It is
clear enough without this that the contribu-

tion of Protestantism to modern economic development, which is, in point of fact, one of the most characteristic features of our modern world, is to be ascribed, not to Protestantism as a whole, but primarily to Calvinism, Pietism, and the Sectaries, and that even with them this contribution is only an indirect and consequently an involuntary one. Above all, the imposing but also terrible expansion of modern capitalism, with its calculating coldness and soullessness, its unscrupulous greed and pitilessness, its turning to gain for gain's sake, to fierce and ruthless competition, its agonising lust of victory, its blatant satisfaction in the tyrannical power of the merchant class, has entirely loosed it from its former ethical foundation; and it has become a power directly opposed to genuine Calvinism and Protestantism. When it no longer practises asceticism for the honour of God, but for the gaining of power, to the honour of man, it has no longer anything in common with Protestantism except its

strongly individualistic spirit, now no longer
held in check by the social and religious
spirit of early Calvinism. It is, in fact, the
fate of the "intra-mundane" asceticism that,
having once accorded recognition to work and
life in the world, while not ascribing to them
an inwardly essential ethical value, it can
never again get rid of the horde of spirits
which swarms out upon it in overwhelming
strength from that world which it at once
recognises and ignores. In the "intra-
mundane" asceticism the world and heaven
were at odds; and in the struggle the world
has proved the stronger. Consequently, the
ethical theories also which to-day support
the capitalistic organisation of life have, to a
great extent, become dominated by a religiously indifferent utilitarianism. For Protestantism itself, in all its forms, the ethical
attitude towards the situation created by
capitalism has become a difficult problem,
to the solution of which the ethico-economic
teachings of the Reformation can contribute

little. Even within the domain of Anglo-Saxon Calvinism, the problem begins to be felt, in face of a completely secularised capitalism. It was, indeed, precisely here, where the development had proceeded furthest, that the counter-movement of Christian Socialism first arose.[1]

[1] *Cf.* the essay of Weber, already referred to, which, moreover, in addition to this thesis, contains much of value for the historian of civilisation. It has been attacked in the essays of Rachfahl mentioned above. To these Weber has replied in the *Archiv für Sozialwissenschaft*, "Antikritisches zum 'Geist' des Kapitalismus" (xxx.), and "Antikritisches Schlusswort zum Geist des Kapitalismus" (xxxi.). Rachfahl understands by capitalism mainly rich people and those who desire to become so. He finds no difficulty about that, and, to explain it, he sees no need of any particular spirit, not to say of a spirit of capitalism. Above all, religion—the influence of which in non-religious matters he rates very low, while he finds no difficulty in drawing the line between religious and non-religious—has nothing to do with it. At the very most its influence is negative, inasmuch as toleration, as the breaking-down of religious walls of division, makes possible free exchange and does away with religious obstacles. But in taking up this attitude Rachfahl fails to consider that everything depends on the question who it is that benefits by the toleration. For it is for the most part just Calvinists, Sectaries, and Jews. On the other hand, a work which has also an important bearing on our subject is Sombart's

This brings us into contact with another department of civilisation, social life and social stratification. It is, of course, common knowledge that the immense increase of population, modern economic conditions, democratic movements, and the formation of the great military bureaucratic States here quite predominantly determine the character of the modern world. Has Protestantism any considerable significance in connexion with these transformations? To this, one may simply answer: Directly, it has none. What it has

Die Juden und das Wirtschaftsleben, 1911. Here Weber's method is instructively applied to Judaism. I believe, nevertheless, that the actual importance of Judaism is here greatly overestimated, that the special character of Jewish capitalism as directed mainly to trade and money-lending, in contrast with the civic, industrial capitalism, is not sufficiently emphasised, and that the relations between Jewish religion and economic ethics are not grasped with sufficient thoroughness. What is certainly wrong is the simple identification of Puritan and Jewish religion and their economic ethics. Here the causes and effects are different in the two cases, and the connection is a very complicated one. *Cf.* my *Soziallehren.* On the present position of Protestant economic ethics in America, see Rauschenbusch, *Christianity and the Social Crisis,* 1909.

here effected, it has effected indirectly and
involuntarily, by doing away with old restrictions, and favouring the developments which
we have already characterised in detail. It
was, in essence and origin, not a social but
a religious movement, though, of course, the
social and political struggles and aspirations
of the time contributed in no small degree
to its establishment and progress. Social
reorganisations of any importance were only
desired by the small Anabaptist groups, but
for that very reason, these were cruelly ex-
tirpated by the representatives of the hitherto
existing Christian society. Their very principle
of the independence of the Church appeared
destructive of the indispensable unity of the
social body. The Protestantism of the great
Confessions was on its part essentially conservative, and scarcely recognised the existence
of social problems as such. Even the
" Christian Socialism " of Geneva was only
charitable aid within the existing social framework and with the means already existing.

Apart from this, Protestantism in the main left things to take their course, after breaking down the forms—for the most part, elastic and prudently designed enough — in which the medieval Church had endeavoured to confine them.   In its influence on the family and law, on politics and economics, in its recognition of the modern independent State, the official class, and the military organisation which Calvinism especially, in its great international policy, approved and filled with its spirit of heroism for the honour of God, there lies also a recognition of the new social world which was coming into being.   But the connexion is here not immediate but indirect.   An immediate alteration of the social class-system appears only in the suppression of monasticism, with all its social and economic functions and influences.   And the substitution, for the celibate hierarchic priesthood, of the Protestant citizen-pastor and his household, with their very considerable influence, is in itself a not unimportant modification.   How far the

Protestant sex-ethic influenced the increase of population has not, so far as I know, been investigated.

It would signify a very much more important influencing of the social system if it were true that the raising up of a class of educated men out of the general mass of the people—that important characteristic of modern social history — is to be brought into connexion with Protestantism. Here, by a common intellectual level, a common school education, and a common educated language, all kinds of differences due to ancient class divisions are bridged over, and by the constitution of a whole social group on the basis of general equality of intellectual capacity, a new social phenomenon has in fact been created; as this, for many reasons, is only possible for a limited circle, it is precisely the cause of the gulf, unknown to the Middle Ages, between the educated and the uneducated. There is, in point of fact, much in favour of connecting this with Protestantism. A religion of

10

faith, which has its centre not in a cultus
appealing to the imagination but in clear
doctrinal ideas, must make knowledge and
education a universal concern of mankind,
and by community in this main interest
overcome other distinctions.   In this sense
Protestantism did, in fact, form an alliance
with a Humanism which had become associated with the Church, and displayed a noble
activity in the founding of schools, and its
educational zeal has given to the nations a
greater and more individual alertness of mind.
But this, for the most part, benefited only the
members of the learned professions, which
already in any case formed a distinct social
class, and education generally had for its
aims in the main only religious instruction
and formal literacy.   Beyond that, it was
predominantly Latin and non-popular.   So
on this side also its influence must not be
exaggerated.   The transference of the ideal
of mankind to the enlightened, capable, well-
informed man, the bridging-over of all dis-

tinctions by community of knowledge, the
elevation of the people by means of knowledge
to a share in the general benefits of civilisation—all this was, it must be admitted, first
effected in the period of Illuminism. Indeed,
just this displacement of the purely religious
basis of solidarity in favour of the intellectual
basis of common means of education and
common possession of education, was the
characteristic feature of that period. No
doubt the fact that this Illuminism took
on an educational character and tended to
form a new educated class, is, especially in
Germany, connected with the scholastic and
intellectualistic development of Protestantism,
whereas in the Catholic districts enlightenment
and culture were left more to free reception
through literature and personal communication.[1]

It is a separate question what significance

[1] *Cf.* Wittich, *Deutsche und französische Kultur im Elsass*,
Strasburg, 1900.   Here are to be found some penetrating
observations regarding Catholic and Protestant culture.

the Protestant sectaries, the Anabaptists, and the later Baptists, Quakerism, Methodism, Pietism, down to the modern sects and fellowship movements, have had for the elevation of the middle and lower classes, for their becoming imbued with democratic ideas and modern economic views, for the development of the multiplicity of unions and associations, the general mobility of society, the upward movement of the masses, and the gathering of influential voluntary associations. With their expansion into great societies, recognised and tolerated by the State, their original radicalism has become toned down into a sober citizenship. That they have played a large part in the creation of the middle classes of the towns in England and America is beyond question. On the Continent, also, down to the present day, Sectarianism has a noteworthy influence in this connexion. But it is as yet quite impossible to define the extent and character of this influence. Here the questions have only just been put,

and the answers can only follow the most
general lines.[1]

The influence of Protestantism on the social
structure and the formation of classes is therefore, so far as it exists at all, mainly indirect
and unconscious.   That is not to be wondered
at in a movement which is in essence religious,
and it is true of Christianity in general.   But
it is a different matter when we turn to the
theoretic ethical and metaphysical conception
of society, and of the relation between the
community and the individual, organisation
and freedom.   This is the proper sphere of
the social significance of a religious movement, and here there are in fact important
influences of Protestantism to be traced.   It
has indeed been described, in terms, sometimes of censure, sometimes of admiration, as
the parent of the Individualism which is
characteristic of the modern world.   But as a

[1] Some indications will be found in the essays of Weber
cited above, and in his article on " Kirchen und Sekten in
Nordamerika," in the *Christliche Welt,* 1906.

matter of fact, in this case also, things are
very complicated.   It is of course beyond
question that its strong religious Individualism,
which, however, was only the continuation of
an aspect of mysticism and late-medieval lay
religion, had a quite extraordinary significance
for the arising of modern Individualism.
And the demolition of the authority of the
Roman Church, which had embraced the
whole world in its organisation, combined
with its own difficulties in the organisation of
a Church authority, destroyed the prototypal
form of the conception of life as dominated
by authority.   Nevertheless, in its view of the
relation of the individual to the community,
which is here fundamental, Protestantism is
very far from being individualistic and non-
authoritative.   On the contrary, in all its
main branches, it is surprisingly conservative.
It nowhere recognises—except in the radical
Anabaptist groups—the idea of equality, and
nowhere preaches the free shaping of society
by individuals at their discretion.   If equality

ever existed, it existed, according to Protestantism, only in the state of innocence in
Paradise. In the present sinful world, at any
rate, there can be no question of it. It is true
that, before God, all men are equal, but only
as sinners and recipients of mercy; the sense
of equality does not extend its influence
beyond the fundamental religious sentiment.
Apart from this, the inequalities which have
arisen in the natural social process are willed
by God; and by their call for mutual service, for trust on the one side and help on
the other, they form the starting - point of
Christian ethics. Similarly, the establishment
of authorities and powers, which has come
about in the natural course of things, has been
willed by God, and these are essentially a
provision for the restraint of sinful self-will
and self-seeking. The revolutionary spirit is
placed under a ban. Only where the honour-
ing of God is at stake is it right to resist
falsehood and wickedness. This last principle
no doubt served as the starting-point from

which Calvinism arrived at the right of resistance, the right of revolution, the sovereignty of the people, and, finally, at the general principle of the ordering of the State and Society by the dictates of reason. But for all that, it only in practice declared war on ungodly and immoral authorities, and surrounded whatever authority was established in their stead with the highest guarantees of sanctity. Respect for the law, maintenance of order, subordination to organised authority, are for it the conditions of liberty. The democracies which have arisen on Calvinistic soil are conservative. Lutheranism, on its part, only recognised the right of resistance in the passive sense, as the duty of patient endurance, and produced the most submissive attitude possible towards authority. Individualism remains everywhere of an essentially religious character, being limited to the inviolableness of personal conviction and certainty by any human authority, and the duty of obeying God rather than men.

Only among the Anabaptists did there arise, along with the idea of equality, a revolutionary impulse towards a reconstruction of Society in the interests of the individual, and here in so utopian and enthusiastic a form that a decisive significance cannot be ascribed to it. In the radical parties of the English Revolution, however, it took a secular form. On the other hand, Spiritualistic Mysticism introduced an unbounded subjectivism, using history and human relations only as means of self-stimulation. But it remained within the religious sphere, and only here and there, by way of the identification of the Spirit with the Law of Nature as given in reason, did it pass over into an individualistic rationalism. This, too, happened chiefly in the English Revolution.

Individualistic rationalism, with its theory of the establishment of Society in the interest of the individual, is no creation of Protestantism, even though it has many links of connexion with the latter, or at least with Calvinism and

Spiritualism. It is a product of Illuminism and the rationalistic spirit which takes as its data the equality of all men in virtue of possessing reason, and the possibility of the systematic construction of Society on the basis of scientific knowledge. In such a Society all can then harmoniously unite in virtue of their scientific understanding of it. This, however, is the form in which the Latin and Catholic peoples, rather than the Teutonic and Protestant, apprehended the idea of Society, and they have worked it out on principles and by methods which need not be further investigated here. In the course of time, no doubt, the two sets of ideas have intermingled, and from their intermixture there have arisen the modern social theories, in which the one-sidedness of individualism is again subjected to correction. In these the Protestant individualisation of the conscience and the personality no doubt continues to exercise an influence. But religious ideas in general have ceased to have any dominant importance in these theories, since they have become too complicated in character to be determined by purely ideological considerations.[1]

This brings us to the question of the relation of Protestantism to science.[2] In this department, almost more than in any other, it is customary to regard it as the pioneer of the modern world. But everything depends here upon understanding rightly wherein this pioneering consisted. For it cannot be said that Protestantism opened up the way for the modern idea of the freedom of science, of thought, and of the press; nor, again, that while retaining science under its control and censorship, it at least inspired it with new self-consistent impulses and guided it to new and original discoveries. The most important point is rather that it destroyed previously existing Church-controlled science, and secularised, at least from a legal point of view,

[1] Cf. my *Soziallehren* and my work on *Politische Ethik und Christentum*, 1903.

[2] [In the sense of organised knowledge generally, including, e.g., history and Biblical criticism.—TRANSLATOR.]

educational institutions, transferring the censorship of them to government boards, on
which theologians were merely represented
along with others. In this way it became
possible to the State to foster science from
the point of view of its own interests, and to
proceed on independent lines, when once its
estimate and conception of science ceased to
coincide with the Church's, as it had done in
the Confessional period. Further, Protestantism encouraged a certain spirit of historical
criticism, which subjected the Catholic ecclesiastical tradition and the current conception of
Church history to a severe and suspicious examination. By this it both strengthened the
spirit of individual criticism generally, and
deprived legend and dogma of a large part of
their content of fact, and thus learned to apply
to them naturalistic psychological methods.
Finally, in its need of tools for this criticism,
and of scientific sources of strength for its new
anti-Scholastic Biblical theology, it took over
humanistic studies, and therewith at least the

germs of philological criticism and unbiassed
interpretation. And, above all, in spite of the
emphasis which it laid on the will and on trust,
it no doubt did intellectualise religion, and
encouraged exact thinking and scholarly study.
It thus established the principle of clearness of
thought and conscious reflectiveness ; and from
religion as a centre, that spread to other matters.
But that is the whole extent of its direct influence, and a wider indirect influence was at
first impeded by the uncompromising, indeed
intensified, supernaturalism of its doctrine of
authority, as well as by the strictly traditional
and formal lines on which its humanistic element was developed. The last-named aspect
of the matter must not be overlooked. It
was Protestantism which first elevated the
Bible above all tradition, and hence above all
analogy with natural productions. It first
closed the Canon and strictly delimited its
frontier as against all human literature ; in its
doctrine of the Bible it solved the problem of
infallibility earlier and more trenchantly than

Catholicism.   It confined humanism to the
study of elegance of composition, the laws of
style and the laws of poetry, and to formal
logic and the laws of thought, and in all matters
of material knowledge it demanded as slavish
a deference to the profane authorities of
antiquity as it did in theology to the sacrosanct
authority of the Bible.   The great Leyden
school of philologists was frequently at odds
with it on various issues.   The ideas of a
Scaliger found in it air enough, no doubt, but
no firm foothold.   A Hugo Grotius springs
from circles imbued with the spirit of Erasmus,
inter-Confessional in principle, and a Bacon
draws his inspiration wholly from the under-
current of Renaissance culture, which held on
its way, separate from Church influences.   The
scholarship of Protestantism was a Scholasti-
cism furbished up by Humanism ; its historical
criticism was a polemic on behalf of absolute
truth against devilish deceit ; its general in-
formation consisted of a farrago of universal
knowledge collected from the ancients and all

kinds of curious sources; its theory of jurisprudence was a modification of the old Church
doctrine of the *Lex Naturæ* and its relations
to the *Lex Mosis*, which, again, was identified
with the *Lex Christi*.   It is true that here,
also, the Calvinistic Schools showed a higher
and broader spirit, but that is due to the
character of Western European civilisation
and the stronger reaction of the French and
Italian Renaissance.   In regard to science, in
fact, Protestantism is not distinguished in
principle from contemporary Catholicism,
which, indeed, having the advantage of a
stronger Renaissance tradition, in some respects did finer and more influential work in
this department.   The great scientific discoveries of the age, modern mathematics and
physics, proceed from the Renaissance, and
a Platonic influence from the same source
brought Kepler into conflict with the Church
authorities.   The foundations of modern anti-
Aristotelian philosophy were laid by the
Catholic Descartes.   The recasting of political

and social science is connected with the names of Machiavelli, Bodin, and Hobbes, all thinkers who stood aloof from the Confessions.

Now, if Protestantism in its spheres of influence and in its Schools, especially in the (Confessionally mixed) Netherlands and in England, wearied out with religious struggles, gradually acclimatised this new scientific knowledge, and finally, from the time of Locke and Leibnitz, learned to combine and amalgamate it with its most sacred world of ideas, that is certainly a process of the highest significance, which permanently secured to the Protestant peoples a scientific superiority. It also, as one of its results, gave a strong impulse to the critical development of the French spirit. But it is a very far from simple process, which was accomplished amid the most vehement opposition from the strict, older Protestantism, and only became possible through the emergence in Protestantism of new religious elements— in so far as it was not due to an exactly opposite cause, the enfeeblement of the

religious spirit and the reaction from the
Confessional period. This complicated process,
in its present results, causes the identification
of the scientific and critical with the Protestant
religious spirit to appear to many to be self-
evident. In reality it implies, itself, a decisive
recasting and transformation of the whole idea
of Protestantism, and therefore only comes
into question at a later point, when we have
to describe the religious development in the
stricter sense. The Protestant religious individualism of personal conviction underwent a
process of fusion with scientific knowledge
and freedom of thought. But that fact
also changed Protestantism fundamentally as
compared with its first beginnings. The
possibility of the change was inherent in
Protestantism; but in order that it might
come to pass, modern completely self-directing science must first be born. And it was not
born out of Protestantism, but only welded
into it; and from the first moment of their
interconnexion it has involved Protestantism

11

in severe conflicts, which even down to the present are far from being finally settled.

Consequently, there appear, at the present day, in the philosophy which has arisen out of this intermixture, many elements drawn from Protestant religion.   In particular, the characteristic difference of the two Confessions can quite well be felt in the difference between the Anglo-Saxon and German scientific and philosophical developments.   The Anglo-Saxons are by nature no more pure Empiricists than are other men, and have indeed shown that clearly enough in their Renaissance poetry and their theological Platonism.   They have become so through the influence of commerce, politics, and Calvinism, which, again, are closely connected together.   Calvinism, with its abolition of the absolute goodness and rationality of the Divine nature, with its disintegration of the Divine activity into mere separate will-acts, connected by no inner necessity and no metaphysical unity of substance, essentially tends to the emphasising

of the individual and empirical, the renunciation of the conceptions of absolute causality
and unity, the practically free and utilitarian
individual judgment of all things.   The
influence of this spirit is quite unmistakably
the most important cause of the empirical
and positivist tendencies of the Anglo-Saxon
spirit, which to-day find themselves in it as
compatible with strong religious feeling, ethical
discipline, and keen intellectuality as they
formerly did in Calvinism itself.   On the
other hand, in the development of German
metaphysics, from Leibnitz and Kant to Fichte,
Schelling, Hegel, and Fechner, the influence
of the Lutheran background is recognisable
in the direction of speculation towards the
unity and interconnexion of things, towards
the inner rationality and logical consistency
of the conception of God, towards general
principles, ideal points of view, and the intuitive
sense of the inward presence of the Divine.
Indeed, even in the thought-world of Goethe
and Schiller, which takes up into itself the quite

un-Protestant Neo-Humanism, the influence
of this background is clearly recognisable;
though here, it must be admitted, it enters
into quite peculiarly inconsistent combinations,
and the resultant tensions and compromises
offer the most difficult problems of the inner
life. Schiller, not without cause, held that in
his æsthetic ethics he was asserting one of the
fundamental ideas of the Lutheran doctrine of
justification; and Goethe, in his Religion of
the " Three Reverences," [1] tried to find room
for the metaphysic of suffering, of the sense
of sin, of trust in redemption, and of the
God-inspired personality, alongside of the
poetry of nature and a rationalistic ethic of
humanity—a proof how deeply German metaphysic is rooted in Lutheranism, but also with
what difficulty this Lutheranism adapts itself
to the modern world. [2]

[1] [See Bk. ii. of *Wilhelm Meister's Wanderjahre.*—
Translator.]

[2] *Cf.* the characteristics of Ango-Saxon practicality and
anti-rationalism in James, *Varieties of Religious Experience.*
See also F. J. Schmidt, " Kapitalismus und Protestantismus"

After the question regarding Protestantism
and science, we come to that regarding its
significance for the rise of modern art.
Here, no doubt, the attitude of Protestantism
seems at first sight wholly one of opposition.
Romantics and Classicists have united in condemning Calvinistic iconoclasm, and have felt
in Lutheranism also, that it uses art only for
recreation, amusement, instruction, and representation, and in the cultus, but scarcely
recognises a value in art for its own sake.
And certainly the genius of Catholicism is
much more favourable to art, since its asceticism leaves room for the sensible alongside of
the supersensible, and its cultus appeals less to
the intellect than to the eye and the emotions.
Protestant asceticism, on the other hand, always
takes the sensible into the direct service of
eternal salvation, and its cultus consists of
preaching and instruction. Catholicism is, in
fact, more at home with sensuousness, in the

in the *Preussische Jahrbücher* for 1905 ; and on the whole
question see my discussion in *Kultur der Gegenwart.*

widest sense of the word, than Protestantism.
And, accordingly, Catholicism entered into a
much deeper and more vigorous union with
Renaissance art than Protestantism did.   The
latter killed legend and miracle outside of the
New Testament, and fostered a spirit of un-
imaginative practicality.   That is especially
true of Calvinism, for neither the Dutch
wholly un-Puritan painting, nor the poetic
elements in Milton's Renaissance poetry, are
to be put down to its account—still less so
Rembrandt, who had more affinity with
mystical, spiritualistic circles.   Shakespeare,
too, in spite of the undoubtedly strong religious
strain in his writing, ought not to be claimed
exclusively for Protestant art, as his hatred of
the Puritans sufficiently testifies.   But the
matter has, after all, another side; especially
Lutheranism, and the mystic spiritualistic
movement, have had, even in this connexion,
a real creative importance.   Protestantism,
by its breach with Church imagery and the
Catholic cultus, entirely altered the range of

subjects from which art draws its material, and
set it the task of conquering new domains. It
also inspired art with a new spirit, which in the
end was to reject the large, emphatic art of the
Renaissance with its general appeal, and seek
subjects intimately personal and individual, or
impressive by their fulness of character. In this
way it had a share in the great transformation
by which Northern art turned to the realistic
expression of life, to the characteristic and the
intimate. And, more than that, from its very
centre, from its provision for edification in
public worship, there went forth, especially in
the case of Lutheranism, an imposing expression of the religion of personal conviction and
attitude, though this was confined precisely to
the non-sensuous arts, to religious lyric and
music. And very significant, especially in
Rembrandt, is the contrast between an art of
characterisation and pure light effect, in which
there speaks an entirely new inner life, and the
art of the Renaissance, whether in its purely
secular or in its Catholicising form; so much so,

that K. Neumann could undertake, in treating of Rembrandt, to trace the principle of a new, specifically modern, art. Similarly, musicians are accustomed to see in Bach a fountain-head of modern art; and in his education Protestantism certainly had no small share. Here a religious feeling drawn from history, but at the same time wholly personal, finds its highest expression.

There is just one thing which the original Protestantism, so long as it held strictly to its fundamental idea, did not and could not do— and the omission is of the highest significance for the whole understanding of its relation to the modern world : it never elevated artistic feeling into the principle of a philosophy of life, of metaphysics or ethics. It could not do that, because its asceticism and its absolute metaphysical dualism made it impossible. It could not reconcile itself to the admission of art as an end in itself, as a particular way of knowing God and the world, which is necessarily in some way or other bound up with this principle, and the not less closely connected transfiguration of the sensuous, and the sense of the world as a harmony. That was why it repelled the Renaissance. That is why, also, modern art everywhere proves the end of Protestant asceticism ; it is absolutely opposed to it in principle. Lessing, who for the first time in Germany championed the rights of the artistic view of things and the artistic way of life, had to wage a war of liberation against theology, and Albrecht von Haller painfully divided his life between the two interests. This is also why Classicism and Romanticism, inasmuch as they both have an artistic purpose, are, on the whole, alien to Protestantism and are not able to take up any inner relation to it ; why Byron and Shelley were cast out from English life, and why Ruskin and the æstheticising of modern England signify the end of Puritanism. The Augustinianism of the Western system of thought, to which the older Protestantism essentially belongs, here yields to a new spiritual power which for ever divides the modern world from early Protestantism. It is at this point that the division is clearest. Beyond doubt, in the modern world also, the ideas of need of redemption, of another world, and of the supersensible, will again make their appearance, and neither immanence nor optimism will be its final word. No doubt it will, in its turn, again subject the artistic element to other interpretations. But a trace of the poetic glorification of the world will always remain to it, and it will never go back to the Protestant dogmas. Here, great and wholly new tasks confront the modern world, which, if it really possesses a genuinely distinctive character of its own, ought to show itself capable of giving a new development to the artistic motive, and of breathing into it, moreover, a religious spirit of ample strength and native superiority.[1]

[1] Jakob Burkhardt, *Weltgeschichtliche Betrachtungen*, 1905, p. 153 f.; Karl Neumann, *Rembrandt*, 1905; Wolfrum, "J. S. Bach" (*Musik*, edited by R. Strauss, xiii. and xiv.); Wittich, *Deutsche und französische Kultur in Elsass*, Strasburg, 1900 (pp. 76–81); J. Goldstein, "Ästhetische Weltanschauung," in the *Deutsche Rundschau*, 1906.

CHAPTER VI

PROTESTANTISM AND MODERN RELIGIOUS FEELING

WE have now followed the influence of Protestantism through the various departments of the Family, Law, the State, Economics and Society, Science and Art. Everywhere our investigation has yielded a twofold result: while Protestantism has furthered the rise of the modern world, often largely and decisively, in none of these departments does it appear as its actual creator. What it has done is simply to secure for it greater freedom of development—and that, moreover, in the various departments in very various ways; and besides, the action of the different Confessions and groups has differed in strength and direction.   All it has anywhere done is to favour, strengthen, colour, and modify the course of the development, while in some cases it maintained and even reinforced the opposing influences drawn from the Late-medieval view of life.   The modern State, its freedom and constitutional form, its officialdom and military system, modern economics and social stratification, modern science and art, are everywhere, to a greater or less extent, already arising before and apart from it.   They have their roots in Late-medieval developments; above all, in the growth of town life and the Territorial State, and the great activity in the formation of new ideas and forces which characterised the fruitful centuries from the fifteenth to the seventeenth.   The really leading power in respect of civilisation during the Confessional Period was the centralised French State, in which the Renaissance, Catholicism, and modern politics all united.   Protestantism, when all is said and done, only, in its own

domain, did away with the hindrances which
the Catholic system, for all its splendour,
opposed, by its essential nature, to the rise
of the modern world, and, above all, it gave
to the mass of new, free, secular ideas, the
firm foundation of a good conscience, and an
impulse towards progress. But even within
the Protestant domain the new world did not
come into being without much conflict and
opposition. The English Revolution, and the
American War of Independence, and the
German Illuminist movement, were all revolutions. But all the Protestant revolutions
differed in character from the great French
Revolution; they did not need to make a
complete breach of continuity, nor to dethrone
religion, because Protestant civilisation, by
the religious transformation which it produced,
had already accomplished the revolution on
its inward side. That is the main and essential point. But, on the whole, the important
political and economic results of Calvinism
were produced against its will. Religious

toleration and liberty of conscience are mainly
the work of the mystical Spiritualism; the
formation of Churches on the basis of
voluntary association, and the independence
of the religious community in relation to
the State, are the work of the Baptists and
of the aspect of Calvinism which was allied
to them; while the philological and historical
understanding of Christianity and its archives
is due to the humanistic theology.

But where, then, is to be sought the independent, central, unique, and immediate
influence of Protestantism in the production
of the modern spirit? In view of the preceding investigation, there is one thing that
can be said with certainty in answer to this
question, viz. that if any such influence exists
at all, it is to be sought in the actual central
domain of Protestantism, that of religious
thought and feeling, for in the more peri-
pheral regions of civilisation it is certainly
not to be found. And, taking everything into
consideration, it is surely entirely natural and

probable that they are only to be found here. Protestantism is, after all, in the first place a religious force, and only in the second or third place a civilising force in the narrower sense. It is, therefore, not to be wondered at that its really revolutionary effects are in the main to be found only in the religious sphere.   To understand this we only need to grasp the elementary truths, that religious forces really only proceed from religious motives, and that, conversely, all the proper and immediate influence of religious innovations is confined to the sphere of religion.   That can only be forgotten by an Apologetic which cannot summon up courage to deal directly with religious ideas, and therefore only ventures to praise religion for its influences in the sphere of civilisation ; or by an irreligious philosophy of history which cannot believe in the spontaneity and originality of religious ideas, and supposes that the only way to understand them is to unmask behind them the profane forces—preferably political or economic—to

which the action is really due. But for every
unprejudiced observer the matter really stands
exactly as it appears to do: religion is really
derived from religion, and the results of its
influence are really, in the first place, religious.
Religion becomes a power in ordinary life only
by taking up civilisation into itself and giving
it a special direction. But it always itself
remains distinct from this civilisation; it is
always more a formative than a creative force.
The effects produced by it in the field of
civilisation may be illogical, fragmentary, having the character of compromise, but in itself
it is self-consistent and definite; and just for
that reason it possesses the capacity to mould
other things without becoming identified with
them, and to adapt itself to their changes
without losing its character. The relation of
a religious system to civilisation is always
very complicated. Even the civilisation of
the Middle Ages was special in its character,
strongly influenced by non-religious circumstances; and if through the spiritual influence

of the Church it became a specifically ecclesiastical civilisation, that was due to the peculiarly
complete and logical way in which absolute,
saving truths were built up into an all-embracing hierarchic power. Since Protestantism
renounced the latter, its relation to civilisation
necessarily became a much looser one, and its
centre of gravity necessarily lay in its religious
spirit, which was not directly connected, either
by organisation or ideas, with civilisation.

The real and ultimate question regarding
the significance of Protestantism for the modern
world is, therefore, in what relation its religious
energy and fundamental principle stand to the
religious character of the modern spirit—
whether this, possessing, as it still does even
in the present, a relative independence of the
special forms of civilisation, is essentially rooted
in it and determined by it. The question
regarding its significance for the modern world
as a whole is not, in fact, identical with that
regarding its significance for modern civilisation. For the latter is not identical with the

religious life which forces its way up within
its pale. The ultimate question remains that
regarding the relation of the Protestant religious
spirit to modern religion—to the religion which,
closely bound up with the modern system of
civilisation, is not completely represented by it.
Since the question concerns the present, that
is to say, a complex of circumstances of which
the outcome and the complete extent are still
unknown, the question has a twofold sense.
It may have the sense of a simple question of
fact : whether, namely, the religious life which
has its being amidst, and is intimately connected with, the complex of the world of to-day,
actually bears the features of Protestantism.
Or it can be taken in the sense of a question
of opinion—whether in face of all the confusions and perversities of the actual state of
things, a rallying of the present round the
standard of an essentially Protestant Christianity would not be intrinsically desirable,
possible, and necessary, if the present is to
find any religious rallying-point or centre of

consolidation.   Only in the former sense
does the question belong to purely historical
thought.   In the second sense, it arises out
of historical thought, but goes beyond it, and
works out into the problem of the present day
as it presents itself to ethics and the philosophy
of religion.

Here we can only attempt to answer the
question in the former sense.   But precisely
in this sense the question is extraordinarily
difficult to come to close quarters with.   Here
the possibility of exact investigation ceases, and
in its place we have to be content with a
general impression based on a host of detailed
impressions—a general impression which may
be correct, but whose correctness can never in
the strict sense be proved.   First and foremost,
the question takes for granted that there
actually exists a religious spirit peculiar to
the modern world for a question regarding its
relation to Protestantism to be raised about!
And that is just what a first and most general
impression will incline one to deny.

What is the picture that here presents itself to us ?

So long as the modern world is thought of purely in its political, social, economic, and technical aspects, it can reconcile itself well enough, especially among the Anglo-Saxon Calvinistic, or quasi-Calvinistic, nations, with a somewhat softened form of Protestant orthodoxy, whereas Catholic orthodoxy constantly opposes it with a new Syllabus, and cancels again such accommodations as had already taken place, and even orthodox Lutheranism tends to be reactionary. Indeed, the industrial, professional, and business classes in these Calvinistic countries, drawing their strength from trust in God, and reserving for the private life a depth of inward feeling and a generous philanthropy, constitute perhaps— even in the purely numerical aspect—the most important body of Protestantism at the present day, while the more outward industrial, social, and political forces of modern civilisation are also mainly in their hands. On the other

hand, this same modern system is also effectively without any religious foundation, and
instead of that is underpinned with a utilitarian and individualistic philosophy of life,
which resembles religious faith only in its
belief in the harmony of interests, but supports
even this belief rather on a universal law of
nature than on a religious conviction.   When,
as a further stage, the natural law of the
harmony of interests is in turn replaced by
that of the struggle for existence, similar views
are placed on the basis of natural selection and
adaptation to environment, in which, again,
only the optimism associated with the idea of
development survives as a weak remnant of
religious faith in the meaning and purpose
of the world.   Often enough, moreover, the
modern organisation of life becomes simply a
gloomy, tyrannical fate, devouring all a man's
working powers, which leaves no time for
reflection, and is accepted as a matter of course
without any thought of its reasons and aims,
while recreation from its toilsomeness is sought

by any means that offer. Where, on the other hand, the spiritual elements of the modern world, the principle of thought contained in its whole system of natural science and technical development, its organisation of State and Society, are followed out more deeply, then there naturally appear marked deviations from the old beliefs, or completely new ethico-religious ideas. These deviations show themselves especially in the idealist philosophy and literature, and find their strongest expression in what is usually described as German Idealism, though neither in origin nor in influence is it confined to Germany. In this philosophy and literature appear the evidences of deep inner modifications of religious feeling, but only like the peaks of submarine mountains showing above the surface; they have their being in the dark and unexplored depths of the psychic life of the nations. What is meant is most clearly indicated by the names of Kant, Fichte, Carlyle, and Emerson, with which we may associate the ripe wisdom of

Goethe, which one would fain point to as the
expression of modern humanity in general.
Here the essentially Protestant basis of this
movement is clearly evident, the transformation of the idea of freedom and grace into
the ideas of the self-directing personality
and a spiritual fellowship having its roots
in history, all on the basis of a theism
which has taken up into itself the idea of
immanence.   Moreover, this modern religious
temper, in a thousand various modifications,
has been so thoroughly absorbed by large
portions of modern Protestantism, that the
latter can scarcely be distinguished from the
former.   But it is equally unmistakable that
modern religious feeling is in other cases
dissatisfied with this, after all, ultimately
Personalistic idea, and under the sense of the
iron uniformity of natural law, of the world
as a monster devouring all humanity, or, on
the other hand, of the æsthetic glorification of
the world and cult of individuality, tends
towards ideas and feelings which are radically

pantheistic, pessimistic, or, again, absolutely revolutionary, aiming blindly at producing some change or other.   And where this spirit prevails, all relation to the practical, political, economic, and technical side of our civilisation is often entirely forgotten.   In addition to this, we have, finally, the tendency which naturally arises in such conditions towards scepticism and weariness—the vague pressure of longing and restlessness, which, discontented with the religious content of the life of the period, desires something different without seriously seeking or working for it.   Now that is certainly a picture of very confused circumstances.   An answer to our question based simply on the facts seems impossible.   Nevertheless, I believe that such an answer may be ventured on; at least if one holds it to be an established fact of historical experience, that without a religious basis, without a metaphysic and an ethic, a strong self-consistent spirit of civilisation cannot exist.   If we confine our attention to the actual religious life of the

modern world and not to those portions of it
which are religiously atrophied, it is, after all,
unmistakable that, as a simple matter of fact,
on the one hand an essentially practical Protestantism, conservative in doctrine but not
intensely dogmatic, forms the backbone of the
great Anglo-Saxon portion of our modern
world, and that, on the other hand, along with
it, the influences of German idealism, which
are closely connected with Protestantism, are
the directive forces.   All other kinds of
religious aspiration and imagination are rather
a flight from the modern world than an inner
religious conquest of it, a flight, in general,
from the practical and the real.   Thus, on
grounds of pure fact, we are warranted in
saying that the religion of the modern world
is essentially determined by Protestantism, and
that this constitutes the greatest historical
significance of Protestantism.   The Protestantism in question is, it must be said, not
simple and uniform.   It is a Protestantism
which has undergone deep and inward changes,

and takes the most divergent forms.   On the
one hand there is a Calvinism which has come
to terms with democracy and capitalism; on
the other, there is a Lutheranism which has
become possessed and altered by the spirit of
modern philosophic speculation, and between
the two there lie various modifications and
compromises.   But religious uniformity in the
modern world is simply inconceivable, and
Protestantism is quite reconcilable with this
multiplicity of separate formations.   Nevertheless, it cannot be overlooked that this
religious life has not found for itself a social
organisation fitted to the modern world.   But
beginnings in the direction of a new organisation, leaving Early Protestantism completely
behind it, are present.   Within the Anglo-
Saxon domain they are already in being, and if
they cannot simply be transferred thence to
Germany, the impulse to a recasting and new
development of the life of the religious community—both inwardly and in relation to the
State — is being irresistibly communicated

from that quarter, and is constantly being reinforced by our own continental developments.

To trace clearly this development of Protestantism and throw into relief the problems which arise out of it, is the task of Church History and the History of Dogma, which are concerned with the real inner development of Protestantism as a religion and organisation. Of course this development must always be closely associated or, at any rate, kept in touch with that of literature, philosophy, and society; as, conversely, they on their part have to remember the religious factors in the modern development. Unfortunately, modern Protestant Church History and History of Dogma are still in a rather unsatisfactory condition. They fail to set clearly before them definite objects of research, or to disentangle the strands of other material which have become interwoven with their own; they have no feeling for the new thing which is here struggling into being,

and fail to perceive the breach which has
taken place in the development of Protestantism. Generally speaking, the straight
lines which run through the older Protestantism are simply produced in the same direction,
though partially obscured by a motley collec-
tion of observations on the history of civilisation. Little attention has, in fact, been given
to this department of research. It is only in
quite recent times that a need has been felt
to gain a clear understanding, not only of the
Early Church and the Reformation period,
but also of the present.[1]

---

[1] The best thing that has been done in this direction
is Loofs's *Grundlinien der Kirchengeschichte* (2nd ed., 1910),
and this is, of course, suggestive rather than exhaustive.
In Wernle's *Einführing in die Theologie*, also, there is a
great deal of material. See also the *Handbuch der Kirchengeschichte*, edited by Krüger, section iv. "Die Neuzeit,"
by Stephan, 1909; the same writer's study, *Die heutigen
Auffassungen des Neuprotestantismus*, 1911, and Sell's
acutely written sketches, "Die wissenschaftliche Aufgabe
einer Geschichte der christlichen Religion," *Preuss. Jahrb.*
for 1899; "Die allgemeinen Tendenzen und religiosen
Triebkräfte in der Kirchengeschichte des 19. Jahrhunderts"
in the *Zeitschr. f. Theol. u. Kirche,* 1906; and his *Christentum
und Weltgeschichte seit der Reformation,* 1910.

For all that, certain fundamental features are already clearly apparent. Since Hundes-hagen, we know the special characteristics of the Anglo-Saxon development, the adaptation of Protestantism to the political and economic bases of modern life which has there been accomplished. A growing practical knowledge of English and American circumstances, the extension of our range of vision beyond German Lutheranism, will make this fact and its significance constantly clearer. We also feel the reaction of this system of life upon our own circumstances, and in many directions we are applying to them socio-ethical theories and methods of organisation similar to those which have there been worked out. That is one of the most important facts in the whole of modern religious and social history. How it has come about we have described in a general way above. What practical influence is exercised by Calvinism, the Baptist Churches, Methodism, etc., as thus altered and adapted to modern life, needs, it is true, a more exact and detailed investigation than has yet been given to it.[1]

The adaptation which has taken place is, of course, a somewhat external one. The ideas which underlie the industrial and political groundwork of life have not been inwardly adopted and mastered. But it is only in some points of detail that the real inner opposition shows itself. On the other hand, in the other main line of development, the Protestantism which stands under the influence of German Idealism, this inner opposition is keenly felt and has necessitated an inner adjustment of differences. Here has been formed what may be called the main body of distinctively modern religious thought. And Church History has not been willing to take due note of this development either, in its full importance. It was left to the

---

[1] See Hundeshagen, *Beiträge zu Kirchenverfassungsgeschichte und Kirchenpolitik,* 1864 ; and, in addition to the writings previously named, see also von Schulze-Gävernitz, *Britischer Imperialismus und englischer Freihandel,* 1906, and my *Soziallehren.*

philosopher Dilthey to lay down the fundamental ideas which should here direct investigation. And it is a point which still
stands in need of further elucidation.[1]

In order to make this clear, I must take as
my starting-point the characterisation given
earlier of the religious ideas of Luther.   What
he laid all emphasis upon was the certainty of
attaining the end for which he had always
striven, assurance of salvation, complete assurance of deliverance from the condemnation
entailed by original sin, by the grace which is
revealed in Christ and made available by Him.
That was his main interest, but that main
interest was not something new, but only a
vastly simplified and vividly realised form given
to the old.   The new thing that he introduced
was a new means of reaching this goal, a means
free from the uncertainties attaching to human
contributory merit, to alien, uncomprehended

[1] See the essays cited above, his biography of Lessing in
Dichtung und Erlebnis, and also his biography of Schleier-
macher.   See, in addition, my various studies in this
subject; also Arnold Berger's *Luther*.

authorities and purely material sacramental communication, a means which laid hold on the whole inner man to its very centre with absolute certainty and permanence, and could bring him directly into the closest touch with the Divine spiritual action.   If to the Catholic it was precisely the external authority and the substantiality of grace which seemed to guarantee salvation, for Luther's feeling it was just that authority which was uncertain and alien, and that substantiality which was unintelligible and elusive.   He needed for the personal life something purely personal.   The means was therefore faith, *sola fides*, the affirmation, by the complete surrender of the soul to it, of that thought of God which has been made clear and intelligible to us in Christ. The assurance of salvation must be based on a miracle in order to be certain ; but this miracle must be one occurring in the inmost centre of the personal life, and must be clearly intelligible in its whole intellectual significance if it is to be a miracle which guarantees complete assur-

ance. Religion is completely transferred from
the sphere of the substantial sacramental communication of grace, and of ecclesiastical,
sacerdotal authority, to the psychologically
intelligible sphere of the affirmation of a
thought of God and of God's grace, and all
the ethico-religious effects arise with psychological clearness and obviousness from this
central thought. The sensuous sacramental
miracle is done away with, and in its stead
appears the miracle of thought, that man in
his sin and weakness can grasp and confidently
assent to such a thought. That is the end of
priesthood and hierarchy, the sacramental communication of ethico-religious powers after
the manner of a sensible substance, and the
ascetic withdrawal from the world,[1] with its
special merits.

In all this Luther's sole object was the
attainment of complete assurance of grace,
which for him, while he followed the way of

---

[1] *Ausserweltliche Askese,* the correlative of *innerweltliche
Askese.* See above, p. 80 n.

merit and the monastic life, of sacraments and sacerdotal authority, had threatened to become ever more alien and external, more human and conditional, and therefore more uncertain. The goal was the same as before, but the way to it was entirely new. But with this set of ideas it happened as it often does happen—that the new way to the old goal became more important than the goal itself; from that which was at first a new means there developed a new end and a new association of ideas. When, with the growth of Confessional wrangling, the tyranny of authoritative dogma became unbearable, and consequently dogma itself suspect, the centre of gravity was shifted from the doctrine of salvation and justification, which was closely bound up with the main Trinitarian and Christological doctrines, to personal subjective conviction, to the emotional experience of a sense of sin and of peace of heart. That, however, gave free scope for the establishment of the idea of faith on a purely subjective inward foundation, and consequently also for the

possibility of its taking various forms not bound
up with any official dogma.   The Bible became,
instead of the infallible rule of faith, a spiritual
entity and power of a more fluid character, a
witness to historical facts from which psychologically mediated religious energies streamed
forth ; in support of this view appeal was made
to the living conception of the Bible, which
Luther's religious instinct had always maintained alongside of the legalistic.   Thus an
approach was made to the Spiritualists, who
from the first had drawn this inference, but
who, repulsed on all sides and cleaving to the
mystical tradition, had gradually withdrawn
into an individualism which was without the
power of creating social forms.   Then follows
that amalgamation of Protestantism with the
subjective individualistic representatives of a
religion of feeling and conviction, which now
makes Protestantism as a whole appear as the
religion of conscience and conviction, without
compulsorily imposed dogma, and with a free
Church-organisation independent of the State,

and a certainty based on inner feeling independent of all rational proofs. When Lessing appeals to Luther, " the Great Misunderstood," to take under his protection this genuine Protestantism, he is identifying Protestantism, in a manner which was to be imitated by a host of followers, with the old Sectarian doctrine of the " Inner light," as Dilthey justly observes ; and yet at the same time he is expressing an essentially Protestant idea, as he himself was convinced that he was doing. He has simply treated Luther's way as more important than his goal.

Indeed, the consequence of this development goes still further. For Luther, the being of God, the curse of sin, the existence of hell, were beyond question. What was problematical was only the application of grace and deliverance to one's own self, *fiducia specialis*. For the modern world, confronted with the new cosmology of the natural sciences, and the modern anti-anthropomorphic metaphysics, it was precisely the being of God which was

the problematical point, while, on the other
hand, it was beyond question that to be once
certain of the being of God would be to have
found the meaning and goal of life, salvation
and grace.   In these circumstances, the general
principle of the " new way " discovered by
Luther was infinitely more important than
his special dogmatic goal.   This "way" contained in itself the actual goal, assurance of
the existence of God, escape from finitude into
infinitude and the super-earthly in general
—to have found the way was to have found
the goal, the gaining of which brought with
it necessarily everything else.   All stress was
now laid on the intuitive certainty of faith,
on the inward movement and impulsion, on
the inwardly necessary attainment of the idea
of God in general, on the winning of a purely
personal conviction of His real existence, for
then everything further might be left to Him
and His mysterious wisdom, if only this main
decisive point was won.   Thus Protestantism
became the religion of the search for God in

one's own feeling, experience, thought, and will, the seeking of an assurance of this supreme centre of all knowledge by the concentration of all personal convictions on this one point, while trustfully leaving open all the further obscure problems about which the Dogmatics of the earlier Protestantism had so much to say.   Here, again, it was Lessing who, in his famous saying that the search for truth was preferable to the unsought possession of it, gave a typical characterisation of modern religious feeling, and in doing so picked out just that thread in the web of Protestantism which the modern world is still eagerly weaving into its fabric.   Individual personal seeking, personal experience of pain of conscience and pain of doubt, a grasping of the hand of God which is held out in the historic revelation, in order, having done so, to proceed further along the pathway of personal responsibility and decision to the winning of ultimate conviction, with a calm acceptance of all the enigmas which lie un-

solved along this path—such is the character
of modern religious feeling.   And by its
strong conviction that this is not the scepticism of weaklings but a manly courageous faith,
capable of bearing the burden of life, it is
closely connected with Luther's doctrine of
faith.   In this modern view, *fides qua creditur*,
as that by which God is, at least in general,
reached and personally grasped, is held
superior to *fides quæ creditur*, as that which
professes to know the unknowable, and
trammels too closely the movement of life and
knowledge.   Everywhere the idea of faith has
triumphed over the content of faith, and only
escapes weakness and sentimentality because,
when all is said and done, the iron of the
Protestant conception of faith rings through.

There is still a final point to be added.   The
Protestantism which has passed through these
changes has gained a new relation to science.
The important and complicated historical
process of which I have spoken above, the
inner amalgamation of the religion of in-

dividual conviction with scientific truthfulness
and critical acumen, the establishment of
Protestantism as a religion of culture, in
alliance with science and philosophy, is explained by these developments. If Protestantism now feels itself to be a principle, not only
of religious, but also of scientific and philosophic truthfulness, that does not mean that
Protestantism, as a weaker religion from the
point of view of Church-organisation, has
been conquered by an alien power, nor that
it has forgotten its own nature and fallen into
self-deception.   Luther, it is true, knew
nothing of all this, and cared nothing about
it ; he banished speculation from the domain
of religious truth, and, for the rest, when
particular questions came up used his sound
common sense.   But once the point was
reached in the development of Protestantism
at which the " way " of personal conviction
became more important than the goal of
supernatural salvation, religious conviction
could not remain wholly unrelated to scientific

conviction. The former had to take on the
experimental character of the latter, while
the latter assumed the character of sacred
religious duty which belongs to the former.
Just as Protestantism at this point took
back to its bosom the children whom it
had so roughly cast off, the Baptist and
Mystic enthusiastic beliefs, it also sent for
its other old enemy—and original associate
—the humanistic and philologico-philosophical
theology, and offered it *commercium* and
connubium. Semler, the father and pioneer
of a Protestantism of critical ideas and
instincts, could declare, as an unquestionable
truth, that everything which the newer
theology had painfully won for itself was
already to be found in the great and admir-
able Erasmus. The theology of the Illuminist
period was indistinguishable from Socinianism
and Arminianism. Kant, Fichte, and Hegel
could hold that they were only formulating
philosophically the fundamental idea of the
Reformation. Goethe at the Reformation

Festival [of 1817] could suppose that he was
at one with Luther in protesting against all
obscurantism and clericalism. It is true that
in the present day this opinion has, in many
directions, led to results which dissolve all
connexion between scientific religion and
Christianity, but the combination of religion
with a scientific spirit in the religious circles
of the modern world—and it is of these only
that we are here speaking—is nevertheless
something which has really grown out of the
development of Protestantism. Inexpressibly
difficult as are the problems which this amalgamation has brought upon the men of to-day,
and distant as their solution may appear to
many who deplore the religious distraction
and discouragement of the present, pressingly
as we stand in need of a firmer grasp of the
objective point of support which is sought in
religious subjectivity, dubious as the mixture
of the scientific and religious movements in
some respects is; if we look simply at the
actual causal connexion, Protestantism is

certainly an important agency in this transformation of modern religious feeling, with
all its struggle and pain.

Taking it all in all, we may fairly say that
the religion of personal conviction and conscience, basing itself upon history, but not
petrifying history into dogma, is the form
of religion which is homogeneous with and
adapted to modern individualistic civilisation,
without, however, possessing in detail any very
close connexion with the creations of the latter.
It is true that in the measure in which this
homogeneity is recognised and developed its
own character is changed, and it becomes involved in the most difficult tasks, the accom-
plishment of which is still far out of sight.

It may, no doubt, be objected that such a
conception of the religious position in the
modern world is no longer a real judgment
of fact, but a conception bringing into relief
those tendencies of the modern development
which are held to be the stronger and more
valuable.   Or, again, it may be said that

the actual position is altogether irrelevant; it is not a question to be decided by counting heads; such questions are inherently only capable of being answered by judgments of value which isolate out of the present that element which they regard as the most fundamental and as possessing the best inherent justification, and so offer it as a basis of action, to serve as the central principle by which to shape the situation. It may be so; but if so, it no longer has a place within the limits of this inquiry.

For this inquiry is only concerned to show the causal connexion between Protestantism and the modern world, so far as such a connexion actually exists. It has not aimed at providing a basis for any judgment of value, whether in reference to modern civilisation or to Protestantism. What we have had to do with is simply the actual significance of Protestantism for the arising of modern civilisation, including its religious elements, not the provision of a norm for its present-

day existence, maintenance, or development.
Nor do I wish to bring in such a judgment
even here at the close. That would be a
very far-reaching undertaking, and outside
the scope of our present purpose. There is
only one thing which I should like to point
out in this connexion, and this certainly
seems to me to result directly from our investigation. Modern civilisation is certainly
characterised by an extraordinary extension
and intensification of the thought of freedom
and personality, and we regard this as its
most valuable feature. This thought has, in
consequence of a special conjunction of circumstances, spontaneously developed in all
departments of life, and the one thing that
Protestantism has contributed to it is an
extraordinarily strong religious and metaphysical foundation, which, moreover, exists
independently of it. The question arises
whether this conjunction of circumstances,
with the favourable soil which it provided for
the idea of freedom, will be able to maintain

itself permanently. That is hardly likely to be the case. Our economic development is rather tending in the direction of a new bondage, and the great military and bureaucratic States, in spite of all their parliaments, are not wholly favourable to the spirit of liberty. Whether our science, which is falling entirely into the hands of specialists, our philosophy, exhausted by a feverish attempt to test all standpoints, and our art, with its tendency to foster over-sensibility, are more favourable to it, there is good reason to doubt. There remains, as a stand-by for the coming days of the oppression and decline of freedom, that which has given to the whole fabric a goodly portion of its strength—the religious metaphysic of freedom and of a faith based on personal conviction; which has established freedom upon a foundation which an all-too-human humanism [1] cannot destroy, upon

[1] [*Allzu menschliche Menschlichkeit.* "Humanism" not here, of course, with the historical reference to a certain form of culture, but in the sense of making man the be-all and end-all of one's philosophy of life.—TRANSLATOR.]

faith in God as the power whence freedom and personality come to us; namely, Protestantism. I may therefore be permitted—at least if my personal view of the situation is correct—to offer by way of conclusion this suggestion: Let us jealously preserve that principle of freedom which draws its strength from a religious metaphysic; otherwise the cause of freedom and personality may well be lost in the very moment when we are boasting most loudly of our allegiance to it, and of our progress in this direction.

INDEX